Wandering Back-Roads West Virginia

with Carl E. Feather

*Volume I of the
Wandering Back-Roads West Virginia with Carl E. Feather series*

Feather
Cottage
Media

Published by The Feather Cottage
6 Seaford Lane, Bruceton Mills WV 26525
thefeathercottage.com / carl@thefeathercottage.com

ISBN 978-1-7330460-5-3 (paperback edition)
Library of Congress Control Number: 2024903745

GOLDENSEAL magazine is a publication of the West Virginia Department of Arts, Culture & History, The Cultural Center, 1900 Kanawha Blvd. E., Charleston WV 25305-0300
Coca-Cola is a trademark of The Coca-Cola Company
Wheeling Nailers is a trademark of the professional ECHL ice hockey team based in Wheeling, W.Va.
WesBanco is a trademark of WesBanco Bank, Inc.

Printed and bound in USA
First printing, February 2024

AI was not used to produce the contents of this book.
All photos in this book, unless otherwise attributed, are by the author, Carl E. Feather, and copyrighted.

Front cover photo: Pretzel farm, Hobart Benson Road, Preston County
Back cover credit, author with Red O'Dell at Coalwood: Barbara J. Hopkins

Other books by Carl E. Feather

Mountain People in a Flat Land:
Appalachian Migration to Northeast Ohio, 1940-1965
Ohio University Press

Covered Bridges of Ashtabula County, Ohio
Hidden History of Ashtabula County, Ohio
Arcadia

Ashtabula County: A Field Guide

Ashtabula Harbor, Ohio:
A History of the World's Greatest Iron Ore Receiving Port

Pleasure Grounds: 150 Years of Geneva-on-the-Lake,
Ohio's First Summer Resort

My Fathers' Land: Palatinate Immigration
to North-Central West Virginia

Wandering Back-Roads West Virginia (4 volumes)

Wandering Tucker County, West Virginia (2025)

Wandering Route 50, West Virginia (2026)

A Gathering of Feathers (Lenox Memorial Cemetery Feather burials)

Feather Cottage Media

Order Feather Cottage Media books online at
books.by/feather-cottage-media

Dedication / In Memory

To the marriage partners and dogs
who wandered the highways and byways with me—
thank you for your patience and the bittersweet memories.

In memory of all the fine folks I've interviewed, photographed,
and became friends with as I traveled these back roads.

Contents

Introduction

I have wandered West Virginia most of my seventy years, first as an embryo in my Tucker County mother, then as a child in the rear seat of my parents' and grandparents' vehicles. My parents, who migrated to Ashtabula County, Ohio, when I was just starting to walk, always referred to the state as "home." We returned there frequently, and I always felt as if I was indeed home when Dad's 1963 Falcon ascended Backbone Mountain.

Since adulthood and my realization that a documentarian's work best suits my hands and personality, I have wandered along these ridges and through these valleys looking for that eccentric character or piece of history worthy of a few thousand words and a roll or two of 35mm Ilford Delta film. The rich and famous, the well-established tourist trap, are of no interest to me. My wanderings are for the commoner with an uncommon interest, the glimmer of past sunsets in obscure places, and hand-painted signs or arrows pointing to a snoozing tale. No interstates for me, either. The back roads are the routes I take, and there along find the folks who patiently answer my questions, share their anecdotes, and open their shops and homes to my camera. Never once have I been shooed away with a shotgun, and I can think of only one or two who flatly refused my inquiry. Only one—an Ivy-League graduate—outright rejected the prose I crafted about him.

Many of the photo-and-text packages resulting from these wanderings have appeared in *GOLDENSEAL* magazine, a publication of the West Virginia Department of Arts, Culture and History. Editor Ken Sullivan published my first article in the Summer 1987 issue. Thirty-seven years later, I am still disappearing down single lanes and emerging with a vignette to share with the publication's readers.

This year, 2024, marks my 70th birthday and the magazine's 50th anniversary,—a time of reflection. I realize that what I captured on these wanderings is history. History cannot survive without scribes and readers; I must write about what I know of it. Many of the folks I met and wrote about in my wanderings have since meandered off the face of this earth. And the places they built and quirky occupations they held have been claimed by time and their absence. There is no going home, no turning back, except on the printed page.

I am honored to construct and offer these paper monuments to the people and places I discovered while wandering the back roads of West Virginia. The books will be published as a series, Lord willing and my creek of ailments doesn't rise beyond a gentle, flowing reminder of mortality. This first entry is a cross-section of people and places from across the state. There is no central theme among this lot; it is a microcosm of West Virginia. Future books will focus on Tucker and Preston counties and Mountainous Route 50, but at least four volumes will be statewide in scope.

While many of these stories appeared in *GOLDENSEAL,* others are seeing print for the first time, having dozed on hard drives awaiting the opportunity to speak to a new audience. Some published works appear here in longer form and with more images and details.

As with all journeys, we have both destinations and detours. Sometimes, the detours are more fascinating than the destination. Throughout the book, I have added a few of these detours, snippets of Appalachia that I observed "along the way."

I must state an important caution: **This book is not a travel guide to the state.** It is not "current" in the sense that you can drive down a Northern Panhandle byway and visit Bob Harness at his vintage gas station. These places and most of these people are gone. Rather, this is a record of what I found and lost during my wanderings, a memorial to those people who spun the stories I wrote and made the impressions they left upon this traveler. As writer, photographer, and human, I enjoyed and continue to relish my wanderings that produce vignettes such as these. I share them so that you can experience those dusty byways where live the people of West Virginia. They are fine folks, often quirky, as I am, and who grow in life's rocky hillsides the sweet fruits of moil and hardship. I hope you enjoy meeting them as much as I have enjoyed writing about them.

Happy Wanderings, my West Virginia friends!

Chapter 1

Execution Detail at Moundsville

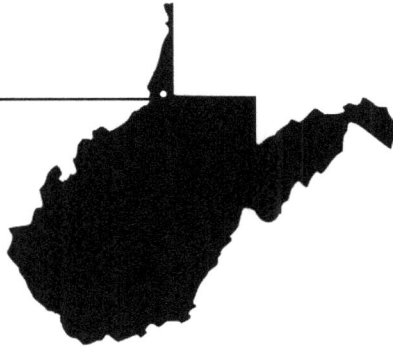

Cameron
Marshall County

I met Robert "Bob" Harness as a result of signage along Route 250 in Marshall County.

It was November 2003, and I was on my first Backroads wandering trip for *GOLDENSEAL*. Editor John Lilly had suggested a quarterly feature that would involve traveling West Virginia byways in search of something interesting. The stories would be a maximum of 1,000 words and, appropriately, run at the back of the magazine.

I'd noticed some things in the Northern Panhandle, around Clarksburg, and in Tucker County that fit the bill, so I took a few days off from my full-time job as a newspaper features writer to pursue them. On a dreary morning in early November, I headed south from home in Ashtabula County, Ohio, on Ohio Route 11 and W.Va. Route 2 to Moundsville.

I took Route 250 from Moundsville to Route 7. It is an unpleasant drive with more curves than a Mae West look-alike contest. In some towns, like Cameron, it narrows to slightly wider than one lane. Perhaps it's the fact one eye is on the road and the other scanning for roadside oddities that makes driving these roads so challenging. But there was no missing the

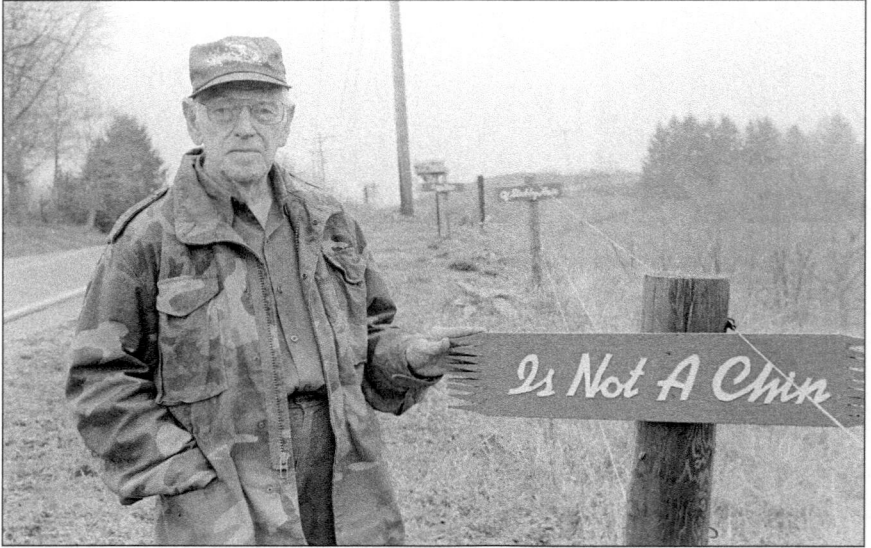

Robert Harness stands by one of his Burma Shave signs along Route 250 in Marshall County, November 2003.

signs that drew me to Bob Harness's A-frame house north of Cameron, Marshall County:

> *The answer to*
> *A maiden's*
> *Prayer*
> *Is not a chin*
> *With stubby hair.*
> *Burma Shave*

The row of red-and-white signs terminated at Bob's 1920s-era gas station, which stood a couple of feet off the highway across from his home. I pulled in the driveway and knocked on the A-frame's front door. Bob, in his late sixties, answered my summons. I introduced myself and told him I freelanced for *GOLDENSEAL,* which immediately resonated with him. Bob informed me that the check was already in the mail—he'd just sent in three Christmas gift subscriptions the prior day. He excused himself for a minute and proceeded to pull a practical joke on his wife, Eileen. He brought her into the kitchen and told her I was there because their check had bounced for the subscriptions.

Rescued from demolition, the gas station across the road from Robert Harness's home on Route 250 once stood south of there at Camp Washington. He poses with it during a visit in the spring of 2004.

I'd scored three hits in a row: He answered the door, he was a *GOLD-ENSEAL* reader, and he had a great sense of humor. Further, the couple were exactly what makes for an interesting story—passionate preservers of history, articulate, knowledgeable, and with a penchant for collecting the past. No wonder Marshall County recognized them as their History Heroes for 2003.

Bob Harness served as president of the Marshall County Historical Society and was a historical figure himself. He'd joined the Army at 16 and became a buck sergeant and paratrooper of the U.S. Army 82nd Airborne. Like most World War II veterans, he remained very grateful for his citizenship and the sacrifices that bought his freedom. Old Glory always flew on the pole in his front yard.

Bob invited me to a guided tour of the gas station across the highway. The frame station, which measured 18 by 22 feet, once stood a mile south of the Harness farm, at Camp Washington.

Bob told me that George Washington and his survey party camped on the site, which thereafter bore the future president's name.

Even the Washington name couldn't redeem the service station, which was near collapse when Bob received a call from its owner, Mike Isinger. The state highway department considered it a hazard and wanted it removed.

"He told me, 'Anything you want out of there, you take,'" Bob said. "I went over and looked at it, and went back to him and said, 'Could I have the whole building?'"

Eileen was accustomed to her husband bringing home whatever artifacts no one else wanted. The collection included a 1927 Mack truck—Bob embarked upon that project when someone gave him a dump bed, which led him to the truck Herman Schaffer once used in the pipeline and timber industry around Marshall County.

In his front yard, under a pile of autumn leaves, was a millstone made from ballast stone brought over on a European ship. The barn's roof was fabricated from discarded steel tanks that once held hydrochloric acid at Allied Chemicals, where Bob worked as a maintenance man.

"My wife says I'm like an undertaker," Bob told me. "I'll take anything." Or, as a sign on his station stated, "Keep the window of the past open for the future."

And that is why, on April 1, 2000, Bob, Jim Redd, and Terry Ashby moved the dilapidated garage to its new home on this sliver of level land across from Bob's house. He and several other history buffs went to work restoring and furnishing the building with materials from other old structures in the region. Half of the wainscot ceiling came from the overhang of the original gas station. A quarter of it is from the Hazel Dell School. The balance came from the Wolf Run School.

Eileen also was fond of saying that Bob would find a use for whatever he salvaged, like the gas station's mammoth cash register. The register came from a Winn Ridge filling station that had broken into; when the intruders discovered that the cash citadel refused to surrender its contents, they ditched the machine behind the station. After years of abuse from the elements, the cash register ended up on an auction block. The auctioneer worked up a sweat trying to get one bid on the potential gold mine—the jammed drawer refused to budge and reveal what treasures resided in its compartments.

Bob's bid of one dollar won it. He eventually got around to freeing the drawer and discovered that mice had converted to bedding whatever

Robert Harness stands with the cash register he bought for a buck at an auction. The cash drawer was jammed, so Bob had no idea if there was any money inside it. When he finally freed the drawer, he discovered that mice had set up shop in the cubbyholes.

currency was in those drawers when the device was stolen. The critters also excavated passages between the wooden dividers, creating a multi-room dwelling. One man's junk is a rodent's treasure, his wealth but bedding for a mouse, I suppose.

Execution detail

Our conversation eventually turned to Bob's career at the Moundsville Penitentiary, where he went to work at the age of 23. When he returned to civilian life after the war, Bob couldn't find work in his native Hardy County, so he looked to some friends for the referrals needed to get a job with the state.

"I tell everybody that Judge Calhoun, Prosecuting Attorney Buddy Bean, and Sheriff Angus Mathias sent me over here to the prison," Bob said, referring to those connections that brought him a job with Moundsville Penitentiary.

Still standing as a tourist and ghost-hunter attraction, the Gothic style,

The Moundsville Pen was still standing in 2024. It has found a second life as a tourist attraction, especially popular with ghost hunters.

stone citadel is almost as old as West Virginia—it was built three years after West Virginia departed its mother state, Virginia. Sprawling over 10 acres in the city of Moundsville, the prison's stone façade stretches for three city blocks. When it opened in 1867, it had 840 cells for men and 32 for women. It was built on the Auburn Plan with barred cells stacked in tiers inside the stone walls.

On the National Register of Historic Places, the prison was last used for its original purposes in 1995. Years of overcrowding and several deadly riots led to its replacement by the much more modern Mount Olive Correctional Complex.

Standing just 5-feet-7-inches, Bob defied the burly prison guard stereotype responsible for maintaining order among nearly 2,000 of West Virginia's toughest felons. His connections compensated for his stature; Bob recalled Warden M.E. Ketchum commenting that he'd come "very well recommended."

Despite needing political connections to land an inherently dangerous

Robert Harness, who worked as a guard at the Moundsville Penitentiary in the 1950s, stands outside the citadel in the spring of 2004.

job, a guard's pay was only $155 a month. The variety and experiences compensated for the low wages.

"This was an interesting place to work," Bob said. "There were all kinds of people in here ... some of them were not worth the salt in their bread, and some of them were very nice people."

Nine inmates stuck in Bob's mind decades after they were executed for their crimes. Bob was on the teams comprised of guards who were responsible for carrying out the state-ordered executions. His voice faltered when we delved into that aspect of penitentiary work.

"This isn't something that I'm proud of," Bob said. "But it is something that's history." And, because Bob loved history, he talked and, during another visit, led me and my wife on a tour of the penitentiary. Paul Kirby, who was warden at the prison when it closed in 1995, told me during that tour that, to the best of knowledge, Bob was the last living guard from the pen's era of executions.

The state executed 94 men there, beginning with Shep Caldwell of McDowell County in 1899 and ending with Elmer Brunner of Cabell County, April 3, 1959.

"The last guy who was executed here, I knew him real well," Bob said of Brunner. "He used to come in down at the annex, the death house, at five o'clock in the morning and give out donuts; he ran the donut machine at the penitentiary. And he'd come in here delivering donuts to the guy that was being executed. You'd think he would know what could happen to him."

When Bob started at the prison, there were 1,730 men and 70 women inmates. An expansion that addressed triple bunking at the facility had begun in 1929, but a shortage of materials during World War II delayed the work until 1948. One of Bob's assignments was supervising a crew that built the addition's sandstone walls. Known as "New Hall," it opened in 1958.

Bob told me that his first impression of the Gothic structure was its enormity, but he was not afraid to work inside its 6-foot-thick walls. He'd gained experience working with prisoners during World War II, valuable training because the state did not have a formal education program for rookie guards. New hires received a copy of the state's rules and regulations pertaining to prison guards and were advised that their duties could include assisting with an execution.

"When you start to work here, the warden tells you when you are sworn in, 'Now, do you understand, you may have to participate in an execution?' And you say, 'Yeah, I understand,' thinking you'll never have to, they'll never call you," Bob said.

Veteran guards trained Bob and established the ground rules for dealing with prisoners, who were required to stay within zones bounded by red

All persons entered and exited the penitentiary through the cage. Guards like Robert Harness were responsible for operating the revolving door or "wheel."

lines painted on the concrete floors. Crossing the line to approach a guard was an infraction, and a guard who played into an inmate's ploy to do so was asking for trouble.

Guards were warned to never give chewing gum to inmates. "What they'd do is they'd chew it up and put it in the locks, and the locks wouldn't work," Bob said.

Inhalers containing Benzedrine were contraband, as well. "That was their dope, Benzedrine," Bob said. "They'd chew that and drink coffee and get crazy."

One of the first manual skills that Bob learned was operating the wheel, a revolving door through which all pedestrian traffic entered and exited the prison. The rotating wheel, a steel disc about 8 feet in diameter, was sunken into the floor and enclosed in a cage of prison bars. More bars formed a wall around the cage. The operator sat inside yet another steel cage, from where he controlled all access and departure from the prison.

The strength and skill of the operator at the manually operated wheel set the pace and fluidity of these passages.

"They used the control off an old streetcar; that's what they used to

Robert Harness points out various features of the penitentiary and grounds during a tour in 2004.

turn the wheel," Bob said. "It didn't have any brakes on it. You started the wheel, and when it started to move you eased off and let it float around. And when it got (to the opening), you reversed it a little bit, and that stopped it. There was a pedal there . . . Whenever you took your foot off there, it locked it so nobody could get ahold of it and turn it around."

Directly above the operator was an alarm switch that the guard could activate in the event someone tried an armed escape or break-in. The premise was that the guard would be told to "stick them up"; upon doing so, his hand would trip the alarm switch.

"But there never was a man who escaped through that wheel," he said.

Motorized traffic entered through the North Gate, the original part of the prison. This traffic consisted largely of work details from the ancillary operations that made the prison a self-supporting, self-contained community. Livestock from a prison farm provided meat and dairy; gardens and orchards provided fresh vegetables and fruits, which were grown and preserved using inmate labor. A coalmine about a mile from the prison provided fuel for the facility's three boilers. Thirty-five inmates worked in the mine.

"They had no problem getting men to work (in the mines) because there were a lot of miners (in the pen) from the southern part of the state," he said. "Some of the men earned their mine foreman papers while they were in there and were able to get a job when they got out."

Inmates also worked in soap, paint, mattress, and clothing factories on the grounds. The goods produced there went to other state institutions and departments. For example, the paint went to the state road department for use on equipment and the highways; the clothing and soap went to inmates at Moundsville, Huttonsville, and Weston.

Prisoners who proved their trustworthiness, and thus became "trusties," worked outside the pen on highway and public-service details. Assignments to the factories, shops, and outside details were based upon conduct. Guards served as foremen of these operations and the various shops within the prison. During Bob's tenure, he was foreman of the carpentry and machine shops and assistant supervisor of construction and maintenance.

Old Sparky

It was in his stint as the carpentry shop foreman that Bob supervised construction of "Old Sparky," West Virginia's electric chair. In March 1949, the state legislature specified electrocution as a more humane way of death. Bob was assigned the tasks of designing and building the chair for Moundsville. His recollections of hanging executions at Moundsville provided a perspective on the state's decision.

Bob was on the execution crew for four hangings: Mark McCauley, Mathew O. Perison, Lemuel Steed, and Bud Peterson, all murderers (Steed also had a robbery conviction). Bob said hanging is a "gruesome" form of execution. "It took 21 to 23 minutes to die," Bob said. "That's a long time."

The condemned man dropped into a pit 20 feet below the door. Prior to the execution, guards used a chart to determine the proper length of rope required for snapping the inmate's neck in the drop.

"You'd go by the weight of the man to determine how far to drop them," Bob said. "You've heard the old saying, 'Give a man enough rope, and he'll hang himself.' That's what they mean. You'd go by the weight, by how far you'd drop them."

An inmate had the job of making a new noose for each execution.

Robert Harness was foreman of the penitentiary's carpentry unit that built Old Sparky, which was modeled after Ohio's electric chair. Decades after assisting with executions, the memories still haunted him, but he shared the stories because "it is history."

"He'd sit down there by the water tower making that thing with a piece of rope," Bob said.

Guards were responsible for springing the trap door. Upon the warden's signal, these three men yanked the ends of three different ropes. Only one of those ropes released the door, and none of the guards knew which rope that was. Two other guards stood in the area where the condemned man dropped. Bob said he never had that assignment, but he witnessed the results of yanking the rope.

"When he comes down through there, they would walk over on each side of him, and get a hold of him. And, of course, he's trying to kick and swing, and they'd just steady him," Bob recalled.

Hangings frequently had an audience of citizens who came at the invitation of the warden or deputy warden. Bob said one of his greatest concerns was how those spectators judged the guards assigned to the detail.

The penitentiary had at least two botched hangings in its history: A

Old Sparky's operation is explained by Robert Harness during a tour in 2004. The mask that the condemned inmate wore during execution hangs on the wall above the chair.

1930 incident where the inmate's head came off and the 1938 hanging of Orville Adkins. Guards prematurely sprung the trap door during Adkins' execution, dumping the condemned man headfirst onto the concrete below. Guards had to carry the badly injured Adkins, convicted of kidnapping and murder, to the gallows on a stretcher, then properly perform the execution.

In the first half of the 20th century, states adopted electrocution as a faster, more humane method of capital punishment. Ohio was an early adopter, 1897, and that state's "Old Sparky" became the model for West Virginia's chair 50 years later. However, Bob pointed out a significant difference: While the Ohio chair used straps to restrain the inmate, the Moundsville chair used a system of weighted shackles for the arms and legs, with a single strap around the torso. The shackles made it easier for the guards to remove the body. Inmate James "Shorty" Vincent designed the restraints. "In a matter of less than a minute, you could (the body) out there," Bob said.

Robert Harness stands with the electric chair used in West Virginia executions at the Moundsville Penitentiary. The author's first encounter with the chair was 1963, when it was included in an exhibit that traveled by rail to commemorate the 100th anniversary of West Virginia's statehood. The guard who was describing the process of execution looked at me and said, "You got that, Sonny?" I was 9 years old at the time, and I swear that it convinced me to be a law-abiding citizen!

Paul Glenn, an inmate, was lead carpenter on the project. He accepted the assignment willingly. "They talk about inmates who didn't want to build the chair. Well, that's a bunch of bull," Bob declared.

Joe Caltabaugh, a General Electric equipment dealer in Wheeling, was the vendor for the chair's electrical system. Bill Widensall, an inmate electrician, worked with Bob to develop the switch panel that transferred power from the transformers to an electrode affixed to the condemned inmate's head. Three series-wired switches activated the electrode; all three guards had to depress the switches upon the warden's command for the execution to occur. No one man thus bore sole responsibility for "throwing the switch."

Guards moved the inmate from his cell to the death house 30 days before the execution. Members of this grim detail were selected by a drawing, held several weeks before the event.

"I had a warden (Orel Skeen) tell me one time, 'I wouldn't have a man on staff who would volunteer to do an execution, but I wouldn't have a man who wouldn't volunteer if I asked him,'" Bob said.

There were 13 men and two alternates on the execution detail. The alternates were in case another guard backed out at the last minute, although to do so meant immediate dismissal. Bob recalled an execution where one of the chosen guards failed to show. A couple of months later, Bob saw the former co-worker in public, and he offered an apology.

"He said, 'Bob I'm sorry to let you guys down.' I said, 'Oh, I understand that. That's all right.' I didn't want to discuss it. He said kind of real harsh, like, 'You don't understand … I sat down to put my shoes on (that day), and my little girl came over to me and said, "Daddy, are you going to have to go and kill that man tonight?" That did it. It cost me my job, but I just couldn't do it after that.'"

Bob agreed. He probably would have done the same thing under that kind of scrutiny from a child.

The execution detail also guarded the prison's power plant, which provided electricity to Old Sparky's transformers. Despite an urban legend, the lights never dimmed in Moundsville during an execution. The chair was the only load on the prison's power source during that time, and Bob was adamant about dispelling that legend.

"Don't let them tell you the lights go dim. When the time came, the rest of the prison switched to purchased power," he said.

Executions were scheduled for 9 p.m. Guards took the prisoner from the death house cell for a shave, haircut, and shower in the afternoon. Inmates witnessed the walk to the barbershop and often shook hands with the condemned man as he passed.

"That was the most solemn time in that prison," Bob said. "Those inmates didn't yap and yell or protest in any way."

Robert Harness recalled the hours leading up to an executions as "the most solemn time in the prison." Decades later, the memory of the men who were executed still haunted him.

While the prisoner was absent from his death house cell, some 30 steps away from the electric chair, guards performed a dry run of the equipment. Bob constructed a tester, a board with 22 220-volt light bulbs wired in series, to verify the transformer's output. By observing the relative intensity of the bulbs as the current surged through the tester, Bob could certify that the chair was functioning as expected.

Each execution used a specified sequence of power surges: "Ten seconds at 1,800 volts. Ten seconds off. Ten seconds at 1,300 volts. Ten seconds off. Ten seconds at 1,800 volts. Ten seconds off," Bob recalled.

"The first one, that's the one that does it," Bob explained. "You know what happens to you? It solidifies your blood and creates a major blood clot. You have a massive heart attack. It stops the blood."

Other tasks performed by the squad were leading witnesses to the execution, shackling the inmate to the chair, attaching the electrode/placing a leather hood over his head, removing the body after the execution, and being with the condemned inmate in his final hours.

The latter task fell upon Bob for the execution of Fred Clifford Painter, a Kanawha County man convicted of murder. Painter and Harry Atlee

Burdette, also of Kanawha County, were executed the same night, March 26, 1951. The men were guilty of stomping a man to death in downtown Charleston.

Bob was in the cell with Painter, Burdette, and Robert Bailey, a death row inmate who was supposed to die with the other two that same night. However, just four days before the scheduled execution, Governor Okey Patteson commuted Bailey's death sentence to life in prison.

The three inmates wanted to eat together one last time, and they invited Bob to partake of their chicken supper.

"Can you imagine trying to eat with three condemned men? Bailey reached over there and got a thigh of a chicken and put it on my plate. And the more I chewed that, the bigger it got," Bob said. "Yet to this day, I don't eat the thigh of a chicken."

Burdette was first man to die in Old Sparky.

"I can remember the minister came around to the cell door, and the pastor came into the cell with me and this Painter. (The minister) said to him, 'Brace up now, Burdette's going.' And when he said that, (Painter) just stiffened up, and I thought, 'Oh, oh, here we're going to have it.' I stood up, and (Painter) stood up, and I took his arm, and he said, 'Let me hold your arm.' He took me by the arm, and we walked out of there, and we walked up to the doorway there, and I set him down in the chair."

Guards placed a helmet containing the electrode on Burdette's head; a sponge soaked in calcium chloride went between the head and electrode to provide good contact and prevent the flesh from burning. A leather hood, with an opening for the nose, covered the prisoner's head. Guards placed a second electrode on the left leg to complete the current's path through the prisoner's heart.

According to the *Moundsville Daily Record* newspaper, Burdette was strapped into the chair at 9:02 p.m. and pronounced dead 3 minutes and 48 seconds after the first shock. Painter went in the chair at 9:10 p.m. He was pronounced dead nine minutes later.

Among those witnessing West Virginia's first executions by electrocution that night was then State Senator Robert C. Byrd, who served as U.S. senator from 1959-2010.

Although many Web pages provide gory legends of death in an electric chair, Bob told me that his observations run counter to these stories. He

Robert Harness loved history and preserving whatever he could of it. He collected and exhibited many artifacts from Marshall County in his gas station/museum on Route 250.

said smoke and flames did not emanate from the electrode's contact point on the head, nor was the body so hot after the execution that the undertaker had to allow it to cool before handling it. Indeed, Bob said one undertaker who witnessed an execution remarked, "Now boys, that's the way to die," as he removed the body.

Bob participated in three more executions after Old Sparky's inaugural run that March night in 1951. Just two weeks later, James Hewlett of Cabell County was executed. Oshell Gardner had his turn in the chair in April of the following year. Tom Ingram took a seat on March 27, 1954.

In July of that year, Bob left the prison job and went to work for Allied Chemicals in Moundsville, where he worked for 32 years as maintenance and welding foreman, skills he acquired at the prison job. Decades after the events, Bob still carried with him the haunting memories of the nine executions in which he was involved.

He recalls the aftermath of one execution, in particular.

"One of the fellas and I ... we walked out of the prison together. And as we were walking out, this fellow said to me, 'Bob, I'd rather be home

The gas station museum and associated buildings Robert Harness salvaged and restored. January 2024.

watching *Howdy Dowdy.*' I never forgot that. I thought, 'How true, how true that was.'"

Bob Harness died December 10, 2011, at Ohio Valley Medical Center, Wheeling. He was 87. His wife died in 2017. In 2024, my wife and I returned to Marshall County to see what had been done with Bob's and Eileen's place. It appeared to be abandoned, and the old structures across the street that he and like-minded friends worked so hard to preserve were overgrown with vines and disintegrating.

As Bob said, it's history.

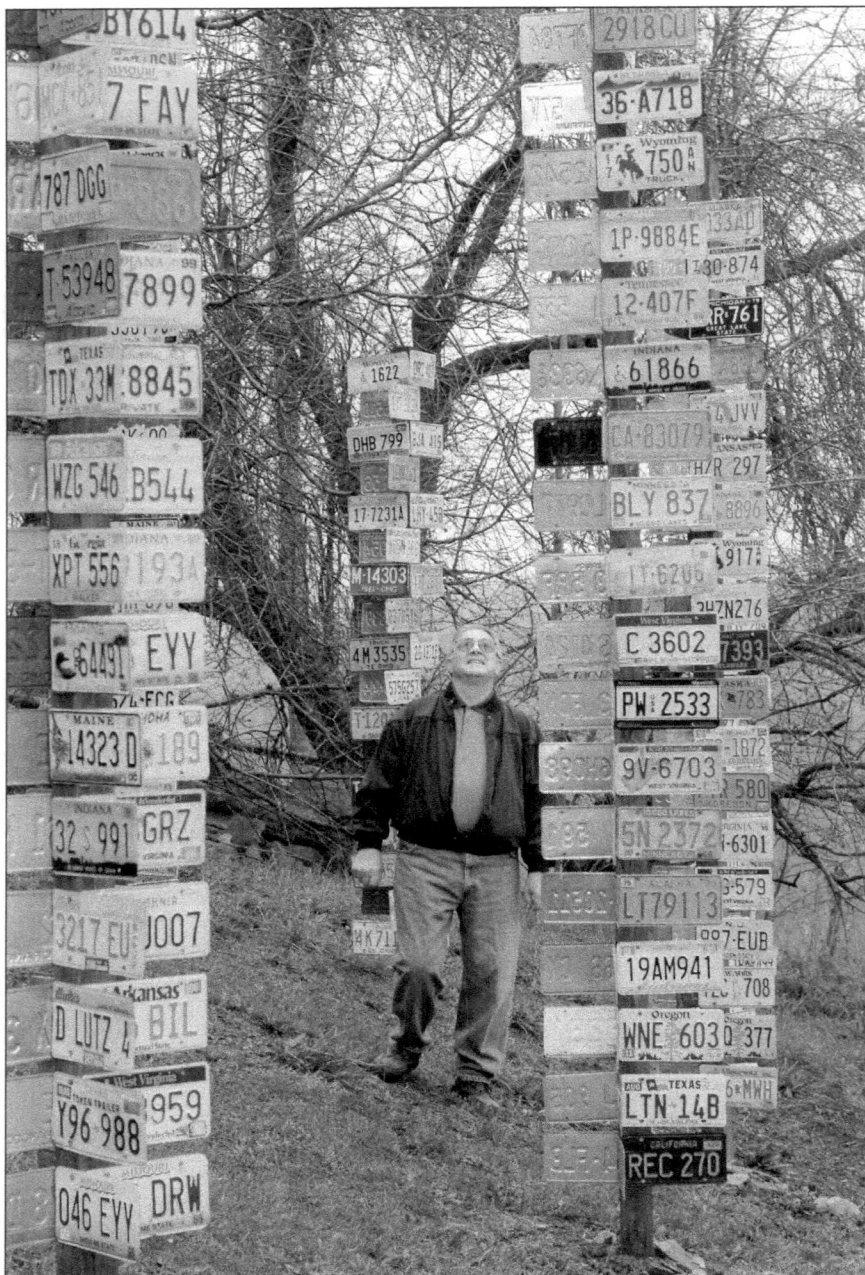

Fred Hammel walks through his license plate forest in Cameron, Marshall County, November 2003.

Chapter 2

Hammel's Forest

Pleasant Valley
Marshall County

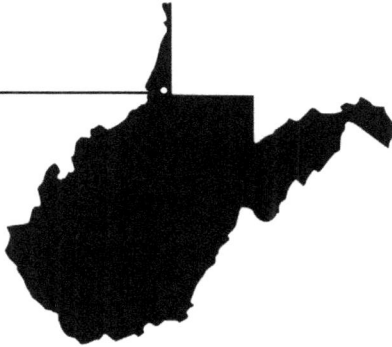

G athering at Hammel's Exxon in Pleasant Valley, Marshall County, was a Sunday morning ritual for a dozen or so regulars when James "Fred" and Jean Hammel owned the community's general store and gas station (1976-1998). The couple eventually relocated the business across Route 250, where Fred installed chairs and a bench for his Sunday morning congregation.

"Some of them refer to it as their church service," Fred told me during the visit that also led to meeting Bob Harness. "It doesn't hurt business one bit to have them sitting around."

By that time I interviewed Fred, he and Jean had retired. A son, Eric, was running the complex: gas station, convenience store, laundromat, and car wash. Their daughter, Lisa, took over what used to be the general store and converted it into a work-clothing outlet.

After working seven days a week from 6 a.m. to 9 p.m., Fred embarked upon a retirement of travel with Jean, who had a career as a teacher in Marshall County Schools. They purchased a 2000 Holiday Rambler and 1999 Chevrolet GEO. In just four years, they put 100,000 miles on the

One of the "trees" in Fred's license plate forest had branches of West Virginia tags, including one from Fred's first car.

GEO and crisscrossed the United States dozens of times. Their retirement hobby grew into a new career for Fred, who served as a wagon master for Adventure Caravans—a fitting assignment for a man who'd made his living selling gasoline.

The Sunday-morning regulars tracked this wayfaring couple's destinations by checking the license-plate forest up the hill from the Exxon station. Fred collected license plates on his travels in the same way other wanderers acquire postcards. He mounted over 1,200 of them on 4-by-4-inch posts, thus creating a forest of memories.

Fred was philosophical about these ubiquitous, necessary metal rectangles. "It's like even though you sell the car or trade it, the license plate is a part of it, and so you keep it," he said of his fascination.

The inaugural entry in his collection came from his first car, a 1957 Chevrolet. The vehicle's plate, a 1958 blue-and-yellow West Virginia tag, topped a post dedicated to plates from the Mountain State.

During his working years, Fred kept this collection packed away in a box. A visit to the famous Sign Post Forest in Watson Lake, Yukon Territory, inspired Fred to create his own forest of "we-were-here" souvenirs.

Jean and the children initially thought the idea of a license plate forest was kind of silly, but they soon become enthusiastic collectors themselves. Jean watched the roadside for salvage yards as they traversed the nation. While crossing Georgia, Fred spotted a junkyard just as the sun was taking its last bow. He pulled into the yard and asked the owner if he could look for plates.

"The man said, 'Help yourself, but you probably won't find anything that's worth anything,'" Fred recalled. Fred ignored his advice and emerged with a Georgia Summer Olympics license plate. But his favorite plate was the one from Alaska with a bear on it. He stopped at a garage in the Yukon and talked the owner's wife out of it.

"She shouldn't have done it, and her husband didn't like it one bit," Fred said. "But I shipped him a couple of West Virginia plates when we got back, and that made it all right."

Although the couple logged 25,000 miles a year visiting other states, they always came back to West Virginia for the summers. They lived on the farm that was Jean's grandparents, where Jean grew her flowers and their nine grandchildren made memories. And as much as Fred enjoyed traveling, he said nothing compared to coming home to Pleasant Valley.

"I wouldn't even suggest selling out and traveling full time to her," he said. "I'd have a problem on my hands if I did that."

James "Fred" Hammel died at the age of 80, March 30, 2016. Jean died at the age of 79, June 18, 2018.

The license plate forest was removed from this hillside years ago. When I last drove through there, January 2024, the Exxon station sold only diesel, and the outdoor clothing store was boarded up.

I hope that forest still grows on a hillside somewhere in West Virginia.

For more than 30 years, Saturday nights were a special occasion in the Grant County crossroads of Pansy. The community's former general store hosted the Country Store Opry, which drew musicians from throughout the Alleghenies to perform for and connect with an appreciative audience. The Western Wheelers was the house band, and included (from left) Wendell Nelson, Ernest Mullenax, William "Pee Wee" Heckel, and the Rev. Ed Null. Elsie Whitmer, doing her Minnie Pearl impersonation (Chapter 4) is a the microphone.

Chapter 3

Pansy's Country Store Opry

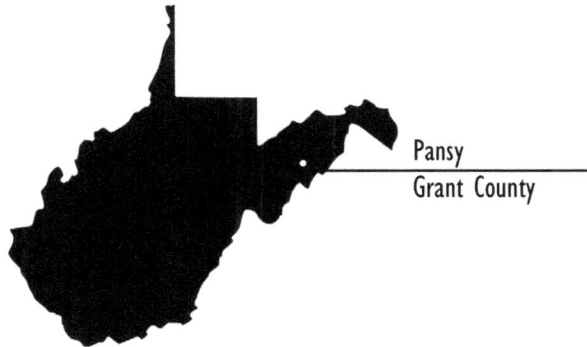

Pansy
Grant County

L ike Bob Harness's Camp Washington garage, the general store building that once housed the Country Store Opry at Pansy, Grant County, still stands. It also is functional and maintained. In 2023 the building was being used as a "family redneck bar," but the opry stage and signage remained intact. It was owned by Mark Mullenax, who operated a car sales and repair business behind what was originally built as the Pansy General Store.

Located on Route 220 about six miles south of Petersburg, this wide spot is an endearing community, if for nothing else than its name. For more than a century, the country store has been the hamlet's center, standing on a graceful curve and surrounded by farms.

I have an ancestral connection to this building. My paternal grandmother, Maud Feather, was a Judy, a Swiss-German family (Tschudi) with a strong presence in this region, including Judy Gap and the Old Judy Church. The former is a physical feature, a break in the mountain range that gave settlers access to the rugged landscape. On Route 33, near the Grant/Pendleton counties line, the Old Judy Church stands tucked behind a curtain of trees.

Joel Judy, a son of Jesse and Elizabeth (Teter) Judy, started the general store. Joel's brother was Adam Judy, father of Daniel Grant Judy, who was my grandmother's father. Daniel Grant was a carpenter and relocated from Grant County to Eglon, Preston County. Joel (1845-1952), stayed in Grant County, farmed, and kept the little store that his son, Elvin Lycurgus (1870-1952), briefly ran until selling it out of the family in 1895.

Both Joel and Elvin had bigger tasks than running a country store. Joel also served as the county assessor and was supervisor of this section of the Petersburg-Franklin Turnpike. And Elvin gave up shopkeeping to become a lawyer and judge. William Harman, who had been a patron of the store, purchased it and did a bang-up job of keeping it stocked with the latest goods. Newspaper accounts from the first 15 years of his ownership reported William's autumnal trips to Baltimore to purchase new stock. Pansy's post office was in the store, ensuring frequent traffic.

Like many rural general stores, the Harman operation closed after World War II. Consumers had become much more mobile, preferring to shop in cities rather than support their neighbors' bread-and-butter establishments. The general store building sat vacant for a decade, but events were happening in the background that led to its rebirth as "The Country Music Capitol of the Potomac Highlands."

The late William Ernest Mullenax grew up next door to the store, in a pleasant antebellum frame home surrounded by a white picket fence, Mark Mullenax's home in 2023. All this was once on a farm that belonged to Ernest's maternal grandmother, Kate Mouse (Mauss), German folks whose genes also were injected into my lineage during my ancestors' decades in the South Branch Valley.

Front-porch musicians

Residents of Pansy and nearby communities had few local entertainment options in the 1930s, before the ubiquitous gray satellite dishes started sprouting on roof lines. Back in 2002, Ernest Mullenax told me that people came down from the hills on Saturday evening to listen to old-time mountain music played by local musicians who congregated on the front porch of Harman's Store. Most were mediocre musicians, except W.C. Harman, who commanded the fiddle and banjo.

Musicians came from the hollows to play string music on the front porch of Harman's Pansy General Store in the 1930s. The building, while owned by Ernest Mullenax, hosted the Country Store Opry.

Ernest first joined this front-porch ensemble after contracting polio in 1936.

"It put me down flat for about six months. While I was down, my mother bought me a guitar from Sears and Roebuck. She paid $7 for it," he said.

The guitar provided therapy for the 11-year-old, whose left leg suffered from the polio-induced weakness throughout his life. Ernest taught himself to play the guitar by following lessons from a book. After he recovered enough strength to join his grandfather on the front porch, W.C. provided him with advice he never forgot.

"He told me time is music," Ernest recalled. "If you played music with him, you had to keep good time. And I expect that from the people who play with me today."

Ernest put his music aside in his early adult life and built up a refrigerated trucking business. His grandfather died in 1951; the store closed shortly afterward. Bessie Harman, his mother, had no interest in continuing it.

In the mid-1960s, while making a pastoral visit to Ernest's home, the Rev. Ed Null noticed his parishioner's guitar resting in a corner of the living room. Ed, a Parkersburg native, began playing country music when he was 9. Ed's father had paid $38 for a Gibson guitar that his cousin sold when he was drafted in 1943. The cousin spent a couple of days showing Ed a few chords before he reported for duty, and with a little additional help from his uncle, Ed Null was soon playing at school functions, like elementary-school Valentine's dances.

The sight of Ernest's guitar in the corner led to a conversation about playing country music. The two men were soon picking together after Sunday evening church services.

Wendell Nelson was the third person to join Ernest and Ed in their informal group. The Upper Tract native grew up in a family that played Appalachian bluegrass. Richard Arbaugh, one of Nelson's cousins, taught him to play guitar at 13, earning him a spot in The West Virginia Boys, a group that played venues from ice cream socials to homecomings and Elkins' Forest Festival. Nelson eventually drifted away from that group, which played mostly gospel and bluegrass, and found his place in county music and the Opry.

As word of the group's talents spread through the South Branch Valley, other musicians offered their instruments: Quinten Harman on rhythm guitar, Sid Rohrbaugh on bass, and his son, Tom, on guitar.

"We got to playing after church on Sunday nights," Ed Null told me. "We would all go down to Mr. Mullenax's home or to one of the homes of the other musicians, and the crowd would follow us. Other people would come to listen to us, or the neighbors would come over. It got so big, we had to sit outside in his yard and play."

With the winter of 1966-67 approaching, the musicians wondered where they would gather for their Sunday performances. Ernest's father, Roland C. Mullenax, came up with an offer they couldn't resist—he'd allow them to use the old country store if they maintained the building.

"My grandfather would be real happy that's what his store had become," Ernest told me.

The building had been used for storage, and it took the musicians three weekends to clear out all the debris. They demolished the shelving and counters from the front third of the building and created a small stage in one corner of the refurbished area. That first fall and winter, they held their picking sessions around a pot-bellied stove.

Wendell Nelson recalled the stage being so small that the musicians were constantly bumping into each other or falling off. Despite the austere beginnings, the Western Wheeler band—so named because of Ernest's trucking company connections—opened to a full house of three dozen fans February 18, 1967. Original members who performed that night included Petersburg county comedienne Elsie Whitmer (Chapter 4) and band members Mullenax, Null, Nelson, Harman, and the two Rohrbaughs. Shirley Yokum, who played guitar, was master of ceremonies. By the time I met up with the band in 2002, only Wendell Nelson, Ernest Mullenax, Ed Null, and Elsie Whitmer were still living and performing.

Wendell recalled playing a three-hour show every Saturday night when the Opry was getting started, "It was hard to get new material every week," Nelson said. "There was a lot of pressure on all of us." Eventually, they adopted a schedule of alternating Saturday nights, which helped maintain both the musicians' and crowd's enthusiasm.

The band passed a hat for donations to pay the utilities and make repairs to the building. As attendance grew and more amenities were required, a set admission charge became necessary. Ernest said they started at 50 cents, then raised it to a dollar a head. It graduated to $2, and by the summer of 2000 had hit $3.

"That's ridiculous," Ernest said. "If you were to go to Branson, you'd pay $30. And we got them beat when it comes to playing traditional country music."

Then again, Branson had indoor toilets and better seating. Long-time Opry patrons point to a little white building across the creek and recall when that two-seater was the restroom. Ernest said WPA workers built the outhouse in 1938, and he maintained it as a reminder of just how far society and the Opry have come. He also used the old outhouse as an intro to one of the Wheelers' corny stories.

Ernest said that when he was a youth, another lad came down from the hills to listen to the music played on the store's porch steps on a Saturday night. Later that evening, the young man was seen standing at the two-hole facility with a fishing pole, trying to retrieve something from the pit.

"My grandfather said, 'What are you doing there, boy?' And he said, 'I dropped my coat down there.' He said 'You ain't a goin' to wear it again, are you?' And he said, 'No, but my biscuit was in the pocket.'"

The Country Store Opry's "auditorium" held about 135 patrons squeezed

Ernest Mullenax stands outside the stage of the Country Store Opry in 2002. His family owned what was built as the Judy General Store, later owned by Ernest's grandfather, W.C. Harman.

into rows like the chickens and turkeys they raise in the factory farms that dot this landscape. Patrons sat in old fold-up theater seats salvaged from an Elkins movie house. The stage was dimly lit by a row of red and blue footlights. A plywood "Country Store Opry" sign with cutout letters covered with back-lighted red crepe paper was above the stage, which, until show time, was concealed behind a dark-red, tattered curtain. The walls were decorated with harness parts, a bugle, ice tongs, horseshoes, and a "NO DRINKING NO SMOKING" sign. More light poured through the single window and side door than came from the house lights.

Despite its austere interior, the Opry had a faithful following of patrons and musicians. "It's just a group of people who enjoy music and getting together for a good evening of playing," said Wendell Nelson, the band's master of ceremonies, lead male vocalist, and guitar player. Nevertheless,

Opry night in Pansy, 2002. Folks put on their "Sunday best" to come out to the South Branch's foremost country music venue and sit on wooden seats salvaged from an Elkins theater. Admission was just $3 a head.

all the band members strove for professionalism and perfection in their performances. There was more of a conscious attempt to emulate the big time shows when the Opry first started. Ernest and the band members frequently went to Nashville to see how the big names ran their shows, then tried to implement that showmanship at the Country Store Opry. During the 1970s, the Opry even had a live broadcast over a local radio station, WELD, which aimed to duplicate the WSM broadcast of the Grand Ole Opry.

"That hurt us bad," Ernest said. "(The host) put anyone on the stage who came in there. He put some bad stuff on there and it gave us a bad reputation. It was bad news."

That led to an audition policy: Guest performers were required to demonstrate their abilities to the board before getting before a crowd. "We'll turn you away if we think you need to go back and practice some more," Ernest said.

Despite the occasional disaster, the Opry stage hosted some famous talent over the years. The late U.S. Senator Robert Byrd attended the Opry and did a fiddle number with the band. Johnny Russell played the Opry on a New Year's Eve in the 1970s and packed out the house. The doorman, Lenford Kimball, became so frustrated with the overflow crowd that night he quit his job on the spot.

The most famous of the performers to grace this stage, according to those who work it, were the Heckel Sisters, Susie and her younger sister Beverly.

"They were good," Ernest said. "They were tops."

Ernest recruited Susie and Beverly as Opry regulars after Beverly, who'd been singing with the Currence Brothers' bluegrass band, filled in for another vocalist at the Opry one night in the early 1970s. Both girls had learned to play and sing under the guidance of their father, William "Pee Wee" Heckel of Elkins, who had played guitar in a square dance band.

"Beverly came home from (the Opry) that night and said, 'Dad, you'll never believe this, but they got a band over there that can play anything you can sing,'" Susie Heckel told me. "We were just tickled with it. The people were so nice. They took us in like family."

Johnny Russell singled out the Heckel sisters for the big time. He put them on the Wheeling stage and eventually helped get them a three-year recording contract with RCA. The girls recorded a single, "A Cowboy Like You," that went to 41 on Billboard's country chart. Fans voted the ladies as one of the top-ten promising groups in Nashville.

Beverly married Russell, who went to become a country recording star in his own right. The three of them toured as The Heckels, but after Susie married Jimmy Franks, she quickly grew tired of being away from home.

"I didn't like the lifestyle," she said. "I told them one day that I was going home." Beverly finished out the RCA contract; Susie went back to Elkins and had five children.

Susie returned to the Country Store Opry in 1992, this time with her father, a rhythm guitar player. Although she came as a singer, Susie did double duty as a drummer. Ernest liked the fact that she drummed softly and didn't drown out his guitar playing.

Wendell Nelson also strayed from the Country Story Opry stage for a stab at a professional recording career in 1971. He cut four records in Nashville's Bradley's Barn, appeared on the Renfro Valley Barn Dance and Ernest Tubb's Record Shop, and opened for Connie Smith and several other country stars. But Nelson traded his roll of the dice in the country music

The Rev. Ed Null (right) and Wendell Nelson were two original members of the Western Wheelers, the Opry's house band. Nelson lived and worked in Baltimore for 30 years, but often made the trip back to Pansy so he could perform with the Western Wheelers. Photo from a 2002 performance.

world for the security of a paycheck when a job opportunity with General Motors in Baltimore came along. Throughout his 30 years in Baltimore, Nelson drove back to Pansy on holidays and vacations to play with his Opry friends. He rejoined the band full time in 2001, after retiring from General Motors and moving back to the South Branch Valley.

"I explain this way," Ernest told the audience. "Wendell went off to Baltimore and made a whole lot of money, then came back here to retire. Me and this preacher stayed here, and we started with nothing, and we got most of it left."

Despite the occasional deflection to the big time, the Opry stage was not a talent farm for Nashville. Its mission was one of preservation. The band played the kind of country music that audience members listened to on their jalopy's radios when they were courting.

The stage was small, the jokes often corny, but the musicians were top notch: From left, Susie Heckel, Ernest Mullenax, Pee Wee Heckel, Wendell Nelson, and the Rev. Ed Null.

"I think if you notice, you'll see the crowd is mostly older," Ed Null said. "We do the country music they remember, from the 1950s to the early 1970s. Roy Acuff, Hank Williams, Hank Snow, George Jones, and those kinds of people."

"The people who don't drink, don't dance, don't smoke, and don't go to the movies come to see us," Ernest said.

"It's like we have a family reunion there every other Saturday night," Susie Heckel told me.

"It's good entertainment on a Saturday night," said Louella Simmons, a Pansy resident who walked the half-mile from her house to the store many a night. "I get to see my neighbors there that I don't see during the week."

The task of welcoming Louella and the dozens of other folks fell upon doorman Edwin White, who collected the $3 fee and, during the show, kept watch for rowdy patrons. It was seldom an issue because alcohol was prohibited. Smokers had to go outside to light up the night.

Edwin, like the band members, was a volunteer. The Opry was a labor of love.

"It's the love of the people who perform here, the love of their music," Susie Heckel said in explaining what kept this piece of Americana going for

The Opry withered and faded from Pansy after Ernest Mullenax died, but the building that hosted it still stands. Mark Mullenax says it serves as a community center and "redneck bar" for family. The stage and signage have been left intact. In 2023, Mark was operating an auto repair shop on the property that belonged to his uncle.

decades. "There have been times that, if it had been a business, the doors would have closed. Ernie and the original group that started the Opry are always there. Performers have come and gone, the crowd has come and gone, but their love for the music is constant."

Even the Rev. Ed Null allocated time and energy for the Opry amid preparations for his Sabbath labors. Quoting another West Virginia musician, Little Jimmy Dickens, Ed said "There's something about hanging your best western suit in the car and driving down to the Opry."

Although Ernest owned the building and could rightly call all the shots, he preferred being one of the boys and ran the Opry democratically. Because of his weak leg, Ernest sat throughout the entire show in the back row between Susie and Pee Wee Heckel, a position he often bemoaned and that front-row members used as yet another springboard for humor.

Pansy would have been just one more wide spot on a curve had it not been for Ernest Mullenax and his Country Store Opry.

"I really mean this, Ernie," Wendell Nelson said at the end of a performance. "It's been a real privilege for me to stand up here and sing songs, and to have you back there."

A weary Ernest had a comeback, addressed to the audience: "You don't have any idea how many hours I've sat up here looking at the back side of this man."

Saturday night in Pansy has not been the same since Ernest Mullenax died February 24, 2004. Pee Wee Heckel died Father's Day, 2008, while working in his garden. The Rev. Ed Null died the following year.

The Opry, finding itself without a home, continued under Wendell Nelson's efforts in school auditoriums. The last show posted to the group's Facebook page was for April 1, 2017, and was a 50th anniversary celebration; Wendell Nelson, the only surviving member of the Western Wheelers Band, was recognized for his contributions at that event.

Along the Way: Old Judy Church

Local tradition dates it to 1836, but the first documented mention of the Judy Church comes from an 1848 deed. Regardless, it is Pendleton County's oldest extant log structure. It measures 24 by 28 feet and is 11 logs tall. White pine logs were hewn on opposing sides to form the exterior and wall surfaces. Square notches join the logs.

The ceiling rises 14 feet from the floor and is made of pine. There are 12 benches, six to a side, that provided seating for the Methodists who used the building until 1910. The antiquated structure stood vacant until 1936, when folks recognized its historic and aesthetic value. Fresh chinking was applied between the logs and a new roof put over it.

The building is used as a community center; a historical marker along Route 220 makes note of it, but a row of trees obscures it from the highway. Travel down the dirt road near the historical marker and cross the little bridge over Mill Creek to reach the church.

Elsie Whitmer on the steps of her Petersburg home, all dolled up and ready for the Opry, June 2002.

Chapter 4

Just So Proud to be There

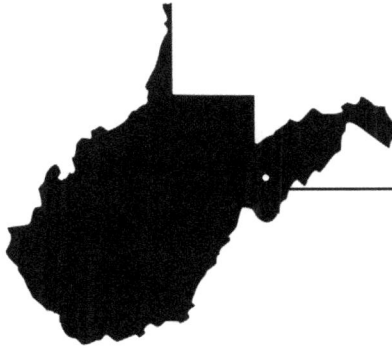

Petersburg
Grant County

The late Elsie Whitmer of Petersburg was always proud to be at the Country Store Opry

From the time the Opry opened in February 1967, "Cousin Elsie" entertained Saturday night audiences with her imitation of the definitive country comedienne, the late Minnie Pearl, aka Sarah Ophelia Colley Cannon (1912-1996).

"Howdy, I'm just so proud to be here," Elsie shouted in a shrill voice to the adoring crowd. "This is your cousin Minnie Pearl from Grinder's Switch, up here to tell you the latest goings on. I was at this party the other night and a young man came up to me and said, 'Oh, Minnie Pearl, drinking really makes you beautiful.' I said 'Thank you, young man, but I'm not drinking. And he said, 'But I am.' Oh my, ain't that something!"

"I just want people to laugh," Elsie told me as we sat in her living room on a hot Saturday afternoon in late June 2002. "There's too much sadness in the world. I want people to laugh. I didn't have a whole lot to laugh about when I was a kid."

That fact makes her role as a comedienne an unlikely one. She was born

July 7, 1911, at Elkhorn, Grant County, one of two children of George Edward and Minnie Myrtle Stump Crites. Was the "Minnie" in her mother's name an omen of Elsie's future? "I don't know why they named her that. It don't seem like Minnie and Myrtle go together," Elsie said.

George E. and Minnie divorced when Elsie was 3. In the turmoil that followed, Elsie and her brother Roscoe were sent to the farm of their paternal grandparents, John and Margaret Crites, who ended up rearing the youngsters.

"His mother took us in, my brother and me," Elsie said. "She raised ten of her own and raised four of her grandchildren."

Shortly after taking in her granddaughter, Margaret Crites was thrown from a buggy and suffered a broken leg. Elsie said the break was improperly set and her grandmother ended up spending the rest of her life in a wheelchair. Despite her personal hardship, Margaret remained committed to raising responsible grandchildren.

"She taught me how to do work," Elsie said. "She wheeled around in the wheelchair and showed me how to do different things."

Things were even worse for Elsie at the one-room Crites Schoolhouse, where she completed all eight grades. Word quickly spread among the students that Elsie's mother had walked out and her parents divorced.

"When my mom and dad got divorced, that was just the second divorce (the residents) knew over there in the country. And the kids would say to me at school, 'Boy you must have been a mean young one'—I can hear them saying that to this day—'that your mammy would go off and leave you.' Kids do that. And so I went home, and I told my grandmother, 'I'm not going to school anymore.' And she said, 'I thought you were really wanting to like school.' And I said, 'Well, you don't know what they do to me.' And she said, 'You tell them they ain't seen you mean yet. You tell them they ain't seen how mean you can be.' So, I did, and they let me alone after that."

Elsie's earliest attempts at performing occurred when she was growing up on her grandparents' farm.

"We didn't have any electricity back then, so me and my half-brothers, we'd put on shows for the kids," she said.

Elsie moved to Petersburg after she married Albert B. Whitmer in 1934. Albert was a painter and wallpaper hanger who built the Petersburg house

Elsie Whitmer at her Petersburg home, 2002. Despite having a difficult life with much sorrow and trouble, Elsie was a cheerful person who loved to make others laugh at life and its insanity.

in which Elsie lived all her adult life. The couple had two boys, Albert Jr. of Oakland, Maryland, and Robert Lee, of Indiana, Pennsylvania.

Elsie said her husband's addiction to alcohol inflicted much suffering upon the family. Not wanting to subject her boys to the shame and alienation she experienced as a child, Elsie stayed married to Albert.

"I don't believe in divorce," she said.

She helped support her boys by babysitting, taking in laundry, and working at Grant County Hospital. She put the boys through college, and they became schoolteachers. Elsie went back to night school and earned her GED.

Leila Keiter, her Sunday School teacher at the Main Street Methodist Church, gave Elsie her start as a Minnie Pearl impersonator. Elsie said the Ladies Sunday School class held a monthly meeting at the teacher's house. At the close of a meeting, Leila told students that she wanted each lady to pretend she was someone else the next time they met.

"We had a month to think on it," Elsie said. "I decided to do Minnie Pearl. I always liked her; I used to listen to her on the radio from Nashville. I remembered her jokes, and I had some of her record albums."

Elsie can't recall the year that she did that first impersonation, but she guesses it was in the 1950s. From that debut in Leila Keiter's living room, Elsie's reputation began to grow. She soon was receiving calls to appear as Minnie at civic club meetings and nursing home gatherings.

"I never dreamed it would go over so big," she said.

Her largest audience was at the Martinsburg Veterans Center, where she entertained at least 200 people. She also performed on a Harrisonburg, Virginia, television station for a March of Dimes benefit. She said a relative, Herman Crites, saw her on television and gave the charity a $100 donation.

Her longest running engagement was at the Country Store Opry, where for more than 30 years she appeared virtually every time the doors were open. She was paid the standard rate: $5 gas money.

In June 2002, Elsie returned to the Opry stage after an absence of several years. She performed twice, nearly flawlessly rattling off her jokes to the amazement and delight of the audience. And to everyone's surprise, Elsie ended each set with a little jig. The band and audience showed their appreciation to Elsie by singing "Happy Birthday" to her—it was her 91st.

"She's had a pretty tough time of it," Ernest Mullenax told me. "Yet she's always been upbeat. She's never let anything get her down. She's always looked at the bright side."

Although the issue of driving at night kept Elsie away from Opry performances, she continued to give daytime community programs well into her 80s. So strong was her association with the character, stranger she saw in Petersburg businesses addressed her, "Hello, Minnie Pearl." And when the youngsters in her neighborhood saw her sitting on her front porch, they shouted, "How ya doin' Minine Pearl?" as they pedaled past her home.

Her shrill voice, country twang, costume, and homespun humor made Elsie a dead ringer for the original. Elsie borrowed much of her material

Elsie Whitmer, June 2002, all dressed op and ready for the Opry.

directly from Minnie Pearl's repertoire of jokes and characters: Her "feller Hezie," her simpleton sibling "Brother," her Aunt Ambrosie and Uncle Nabob, and Cousin Emmie. They were the flawed apples that grow on every family tree, and their characters' quirks resonated with audiences who immediately felt superior to these country bumpkins.

"Uncle Nabob, he was kind of bad to go into town and get to drinking on Saturday night," Elsie said. "Aunt Ambrosie, that's his wife, she's been trying to break him of it. So last Saturday night, he went into town, and she got herself an old false face, a set of horns, put on a robe and hid in the bushes down there below the house. Along about midnight, here comes Uncle Nabob weaving up the road. She jumped out and said, 'Boo, I'm the devil.' He said, 'Well, let me shake your hand! You know, I'm married to your sister.!'"

Elsie Whitmer died in 2004 and is buried in Maple Hill Cemetery, Petersburg.

Grace Louise Carr with some of her West Virginia glassware, Friendly, 2003.

Chapter 5

A Friendly Stopover

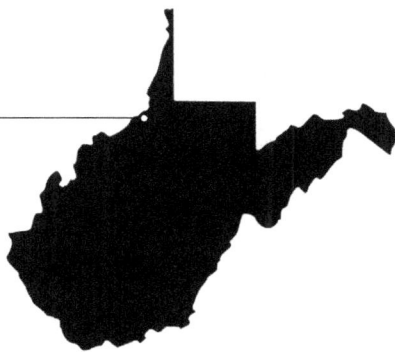

Friendly
Tyler County

Elsie Whitmer made me laugh; Grace Louise Carr made me smile. Perhaps it was because her smile reminded me of my maternal grandmother, Violet Keiper Watring. Or perhaps it was her tables full of West Virginia glassware in a rainbow of vibrant colors that elevated my mood.

Louise owned and operated Carr's Glass and Gift Shop on Route 2 in Friendly. The Tyler County town lived up to its name in Louise's shop, where she greeted me and my wife on a May morning in 2003.

The vases, candy bowls, and other glassware in the front window were advertising and enticement enough to divert us from our wanderings. Louise greeted us with a soft welcome and smile. While my wife shopped the aisles of glassware, I struck up a conversation with Louise, who started the business with her late husband, John Eugene "Gene" Carr. That name struck a chord with me; my middle name is Eugene and earned me the childhood nickname of "Gene," by which a few West Virginia relatives still know me.

Established in 1977, Louise's business was the oldest retailer in Friendly at the time of our visit. With only 50-some households and 130 residents,

Friendly's commercial district was geared toward motorists making the trek between Sistersville and Parkersburg. However, at the turn of the 20th century, Friendly had the distinction of being the smallest town on an interurban route. The distinction was accidental, however: The Parkersburg & Ohio Valley Electric Railways was supposed to go from Wheeling to Parkersburg, but only got as far as Friendly before the project collapsed.

Cochrane Williamson, a Quaker or "Friend" settler, was most likely the town's namesake. If you consume children's/young-adult literature, you know this area from Phyllis Reynold Taylor's award-winning *Shiloh*. The book series and films are about an 11-year-old boy who is confronted by morality's difficult choices as he tries to protect an abused dog. The dog's name comes from the nearby town, Shiloh. Or, if you are a tomato lover, you may have encountered the Friendly heirloom. It is said to have been discovered in 1884 in a pile of debris washed ashore by an Ohio River flood.

Floods and ornery, beagle-beating neighbors have something to teach us, as do abandoned public, commercial, and residential structures that speak of a town that once possessed a thriving economy. Louise's whitewashed block building and its large plate-glass window hinted of a more prosperous prior life, as well. It had but two rooms: a large, open back section where men in blue work clothes once earned a mechanic's wage by the light of 60-watt trouble lamps, and a front room with a tin ceiling where repair bills were tallied, cans of oil sold, and small talk exchanged while motorists waited for their freshly tuned vehicle to emerge from the bay.

Louise sold glassware out of these rooms—not the made-in-China, dollar-store kind of kitsch that floods flea market tables in 2024, but the amber, dark-blue, orange, green, and crystal-clear masterpieces that once came from the red glow of West Virginia's glass furnaces. Some of the glassware in her shop still bore the original factory stickers: Fenton, Viking, Westmoreland. The origins of others were identified by Louise and noted on hand-written white labels.

Gene taught Louise most of what she knew about the glassware she sold. After he came home from serving in the Seabees during World War II, Eugene got a job at L.G. Wright Glassware in New Martinsville. He was a traveling salesman for the glassware distributor, a job that took him away from home several weeks at a spell. A heart attack in 1956 ended his career on the road. The couple and their six children moved back to the family farm, where they made a living raising beef cattle. Neighbors assisted them with the more strenuous aspects of the work.

When the former garage building became available in the mid-1970s, the couple decided to purchase it and use it as an outlet for overstock West Virginia and Pennsylvania glassware.

"We stocked it with glass, and we've been here ever since," Louise said.

Gene and Louise spent many years working side-by-side in the business as they traveled the region purchasing glass overstock from factories and distributors. Louise displayed it in their shop, kept it spotless, and eventually wrapped it in newsprint, packed it in a box, and sent it on its way to become cherished reminders of a little shop and its Friendly owner on Route 2.

Early in this venture, Louise and Eugene approached Weston Louie Glass about purchasing stock. "The plant manager told us they had sold out to Princess House and (the new owner) didn't want the old stock. He offered it to us, but we would have to furnish our own cartons, pack all of it ourselves, and move it," Louise said. It was a big risk for a small business. "We had just enough money to settle things, so that's what we done."

"And where do you think we got all those cartons? We went to all the liquor stores and got all the empty cartons they had. They were perfect – they were partitioned and padded," said Louise, who was a founder of the Sisterville Church of the Nazarene.

In 2003, Louise still had about a third of the stock that she and Eugene had purchased. Some of it remained packed in those liquor boxes and stashed under tables in the backroom. The goblets, iced-tea glasses, and hand-blown items from Weston Louie Glass shared space with Fenton's Hobnail Glass, Imperial's etched paper weights and medallion glass, Blenko's crackle glass, and Viking's richly colored vases and specialty pieces. Traditional flea market fare, such as framed pictures and candles, occupied any gaps on the shelves and tables.

Louise told me about two men from England who purchased one of those flea market items, a pencil engraving of an English clipper shop. The buyers were on a buying trip through the Northern Panhandle—one of them owned a glassware shop, the other a museum. The latter wanted the picture for an exhibit, but it appeared too big to take aboard the airplane. His friend suggested they wrap it in a dirty shirt and put it in their luggage.

Louise said they went to their car, pulled their suitcase from the trunk, and quickly discovered the frame was too large for it. Then they asked if it would be OK if they took only the picture and left the frame behind. Eugene and Louise agreed, and the men were delighted to have solved the problem.

"After they left, my husband and I looked at (the frame), and there behind the other picture was a picture of Dean Martin and Jerry Lewis that had been taken in the 1950s," she said. "The next morning, a fellow stopped, and as soon as he saw that he said, 'I collect them.' So, we sold the item twice."

Louise smiled softly as she recalled the incident of double good fortune. That was back six, seven years earlier, when Eugene was still alive, before the stroke that sent him to the hospital, then the nursing home and, finally, a little cottage on the country property of their daughter, Anna Cooper.

"All six of our kids and their husbands and wives worked shifts to take care of him," Louise said. "They did that for four months."

The last three months were the most difficult, but the Carr children stood by their father.

"He couldn't talk, see, or move, but he could hear," Louise said. "They turned him in that bed every three or four hours. He was very much at peace because he was in one of his daughter's homes, and the children were taking care of him."

Eugene died Thanksgiving Day 2003. They had been married fifty-two years. Between his illness and the grieving process, the store was closed for nearly a year. There was no question in Louise's mind that Carr's should re-open once spring arrived.

"I was kind of glad to get back in here," she said. "I know that's what he would have wanted me to do."

Louise kept a photograph of her husband, herself, and one of their daughters near the cash register. It was taken at Eugene's sixtieth high school class reunion. Like the glassware glowing in the front window of her shop, every person in the photograph beamed with the joy of the moment.

"It's been fun," Louise said, the mist of memories sparkling in her friendly eyes.

My wife and I bought a box of stout beverage tumblers from Grace Louise and continued our wanderings.

Grace Louise Car stands outside her Friendly glassware shop on Route 2, May 2003. The building was formerly an auto repair garage.

Grace Louise Carr died July 26, 2016, at Brookdale Assisted Living. She was surrounded by her family when she passed.

I lost track of the glassware when my wife and I divorced 10 years later. I have not been back to the little town since that beautiful day in May 2003. Like the colorful glassware in Carr's plate-glass window, the world seemed more colorful, sparkling, and friendly then.

Charles Waldrum pushes one of his bicycles down a damp alley in Wheeling as he begins his night shift as the community's vigilante. December 2012.

Chapter 6

Walking Wheeling with Moon Dog

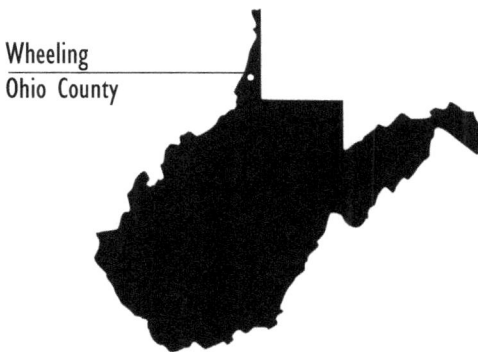

Wheeling
Ohio County

I first met Moon Dog on a rainy December evening in 2012 at Wheeling's
16th Street Convenience Store. You could find him there around dusk
as Charles Waldrum, the legendary nocturnal vigilante, stocked up on
refreshments before commencing his rounds.

Most Wheeling folks assumed that this large, bearded man who aim-
lessly peddled a bicycle around their town was homeless, but Charles had
an apartment in one of the old brick structures on Lane 13. His neighbor,
Janice Reed, told me he was a responsible tenant but played the radio too
loud for her tastes. The blaring music aside, she found comfort knowing
that he was a shout away. "He helps me watch over my house; he's a nice
neighbor. I like him," she told me.

Charles had worked "at least 15 jobs" before he found his purpose as a
full-time, night-time vigilante. He carried a huge flashlight and defended
himself with a broom handle wrapped with duct tape as he pedaled/
pushed one of the hundreds of bicycles he owned in his three decades of
uncompensated service. Two fiberglass poles at the back of his bicycle rose

high into the air and displayed flags ranging from Old Glory to those of other nations.

"I got 283 flags," he told me. "You put them on (the bike), then you can't pick up the bike with all that weight on there. I got another bike at home that has 592 flags on it, and it is so heavy I can't ride it. I just leave it inside the house."

His decorated bicycles were mainstays in Upper Ohio Valley parades. Charles pedaled the ponderous velocipedes as far as Martin's Ferry, Moundsville, and St. Clairsville to ride in a procession.

"He (loves to ride in parades) because he loves kids," Kathie Loos told me. "It's because he's a kid himself."

Despite being a fixture at these processions, in 2011, Charles Waldrum was excluded from the Wheeling Chamber of Commerce Christmas Parade. That made the "town go crazy," said a friend. The decision deeply hurt Charles, who was later invited to be grand marshal for the 2012 parade. He accepted the invitation if he could transfer to his bicycle and ride at the end of the parade after the marshal's unit completed the route.

"The parade is not over until we see Moon Dog behind Santa," a Wheeling business owner told me.

Charles' persona reached cult status in 2008 when the Wheeling Nailers produced a Moon Dog bobblehead doll. The collectible marked a memorable event in Waldrum's life; he tossed out the puck at a hockey game in the WesBanco Arena. Only 2,500 of the nodders were produced.

"You got to go on eBay to get one of them things," Charles told me four years later. "They get a lot of money for them, over $100."

The Nailers organization offered him a royalty, but he didn't want it, according to Sheryl. That's the way he lived; money was meaningless to him, and he preferred to make his own way, be his own person, in a world that rewards conformity. Charles Waldrum was eccentric, independent, and quirky, but not greedy.

The night I walked the streets of Wheeling with him, Charles told me about "a whole bunch of money" he had stashed away in a container and buried in a hill. "Nothing can hurt the money," he said. "That thing is way down in the ground. It's bigger than I am."

Only Charles knew the stash's location, and if it was just legend or fact. He lived as if the latter were true.

Charles Waldrum, aka Moon Dog, December 2012.

"A lot of people out on the street, he will just hand them money," Sheryl told me. "And he will not take money from other people."

If a child approached Charles, he would reach into a jacket pocket and produce a dollar bill for the youngster. He gladly purchased a soft drink for any child who asked him. Children felt more comfortable with the color of his skin and unorthodox lifestyle than those who hid behind their insecurities by hurling slurs at this perambulating target. Charles once told a reporter that the only way he could explain that kind of hatred was that those dishing it out must hate themselves, as well.

"I like little kids," Charles told me. "I'm like a little kid at heart. You can't take money with you, man. You know what I mean?"

Sergeant Bill Nolan of the Wheeling Police Department told me, "Moon Dog has a heart of gold. He really cares about people." Jessica Yost, whose father owned the convenience store, told reporter Steve Novotney that Charles never hesitated to give a kid his leftover change so the youngster could buy candy or snacks. He was equally generous with his labors, assisting at the store and never asking for anything in return.

He was born September 18, 1958, one of 11 children of Mamie Walker and Charles Waldrum. He was reared in East Wheeling, where he attended public schools but did not graduate high school. He lived on a Social Security benefit that he began receiving when his father died.

Ask 10 Wheeling residents how he got his name, and you'll get as many different answers.

"We call him Moon Dog because he takes a bite out of crime," said Lance Miller, who owned Neely's Grocery, one of the Wheeling businesses on Charles' beat.

Randy Link, the city's postmaster, said he was told that the reason he got the name Moon Dog was because (of his looks) and he barked at the moon. Randy, who grew up in Wheeling, was one of Charles's classmates. With bold facial features, legs like oak trunks, and a beard that he trimmed but twice a year and never to the skin, Charles's appearance disguised his age. "He's been Moon Dog ever since he was a kid. I never heard of him being called 'Charles Waldrum,' but he's one of the nicest persons you ever want to meet," Randy told me.

Dick Clark, head clerk at the Main Street Knights Inn where I was staying, told me he immediately noticed this "guy riding around on a bicycle" when he first arrived in town back in 1975.

"I asked who he was, and (locals) said 'Moon Dog.' You just look for him; he's part of us now. He's quite the guy. You'll never meet another character like Moon Dog."

"He loves the name," said Cheryl Small, a former classmate from their school days in East Wheeling.

His brothers, Johnny and Jake, also claimed that Charles loved his nickname, although close friends called him "Moonie." Charles, however, expressed a different view to a reporter in another interview. "They started calling me 'Moon Dog' a long time ago, because I go out at night," he told Steve Novotney. "I go out at night because it's cooler. That's why. But I ain't no dog. I look for stuff that ain't right. I try to help because there are some bad people in this world."

Legend is Charles was once among the "bad" elements, allegedly setting an arson fire on Wheeling Island as a youth. He quickly realized the error of his ways and dedicated his life to assisting The Nail City's firefighters. His familiarity with the city and configuration of its aging buildings proved

Day or night, Charles Waldrum patrolled the streets of Wheeling on one of his many bicycles.

beneficial to the department. Wheeling Fire Chief Larry Helms told me that the department received a call about smoke in an apartment in the building in which Charles lived. As the firefighters contemplated how to break into the locked apartment, Moon Dog exited the front door. He

Charles Waldrum's neighbor, Janice Reed, felt secure living next to Moon Dog. Her only complaint about him was that the volume control on his radio was set too high for her tastes. December 2012.

had gone up a fire escape and through a window to access the smoke-filled apartment.

Wheeling Firefighters showed their appreciation for Charles's vigilance and assistance by giving him bicycles as the need arose. But Charles was fussy about what kind of bike he rode and would reject any that didn't meet his specifications. The city's firefighters also gave him decommissioned jackets. Dressed in the heavy jacket, pedaling his bicycle along one of the city's thoroughfares, Charles scoured the dark recesses of Wheeling for suspicious activity and rattled business doors in the manner once common for urban beat cops.

"I've found 47 businesses that left their doors unlocked," Charles told me as we left the convenience store for his rounds. "I check on them day and night." Lance Neely said that Charles discovered an unlocked business door one night, reported it, and stood guard until the owner could arrive and secure the shop.

A vigilant watchman, he also spotted shoplifters and pointed them out to store owners. "One time someone was in here shoplifting, and he hurried over and locked the door and stood in front of it until the police came," Sheryl said.

"You got to be out there," said Charles, who saw himself as an extension of the city's professional crime-fighting squad rather than a freelancer. "He does his fair share," Sargent Nolan told me. "Moon Dog has been a fairly good asset for us."

"In my opinion, he's been an upstanding citizen," the sergeant said. "He's a very private individual, and it takes time to know him, to get him to open up."

The sergeant recalled his rookie days of walking the beat in the theater district. Charles was observing the activity from an alley, and pedestrians unfamiliar with him gave the vigilante a wide berth. Some expressed their angst to the future sergeant.

"I told them that if there were any person who was looking out for their safety in the city, it was Moon Dog. He will do whatever he can to help you in any situation," he said.

Charles witnessed and attempted to stop drug deals, muggings, fights, robberies, and arsons while on patrol. "I've broken up a lot of fights and stuff in downtown Wheeling," he said.

He memorized the location of each payphone in Wheeling, so he'd know the shortest distance to reporting a crime or fire in progress. In June 2012, Charles heard gunshots near a convenience store at 1:30 a.m. He summoned police to an attempted murder. During another patrol, he saw a female arsonist running out of the back of a store building.

"I told her to stop. She got in the car and took off, then I saw the fire," he said. "She'd put down a lot of gasoline in the store. I told the fire department everything."

Charles showed up at virtually every fire scene and attempted to assist firefighters. The fire chief recalled a time the department responded to a fire on Wheeling Island and the truck passed Charles' convenience-store headquarters on the way. By the time firefighters were attaching hoses to hydrants, Charles arrived on his bicycle.

"He used to be pretty quick back then," the chief said.

The only things that kept Charles from his rounds were deep snow and heavy rain. Even a large, painful cut in his left foot did not prevent him from patrolling during our night of wandering about Wheeling. He wore a tennis shoe on his right foot and a bandage on the left. Despite walking through some rough sections and packing an expensive Nikon DSLR and set of lenses, I felt safe with Charles in the lead.

"There is nothing to be afraid of out there," Charles told me. "I've been punched, and I got beat up. And I take a lot of names. You can't trust nobody out there. You got to keep everything on your mind."

For those who earned the trust and friendship of Charles Waldrum, they received the gift of knowing a legend. Indeed, Charles treated his friends like royalty. A couple of weeks before Christmas, he surprised Sheryl Small and her coworker at the convenience store with ornate picture frames.

"This is my man; I love him," Kathie Loos said. "He's my 'Boo'—that's what we call him. He's a very thoughtful person."

"Someday I'm going to be his wife. I love him," Sheryl said. "But he won't marry me."

I asked Charles why he had not popped the question.

"You marry her," he quipped.

Our paths crossed a few more times when I visited Wheeling, but nothing like that night when I trailed him for several hours through the streets that glistened with the mix of sodium-vapor security lamps and blinking Christmas lights. He was probably the most photogenic person I've ever pointed my lenses at, and I cherish the experience and memories.

Charles Waldrum no longer patrols the streets of Wheeling. According to a *Wheeling Intelligencer* article published December 19, 2020, Charles was recovering in Peterson Healthcare and Rehabilitation in Woodsdale following amputation of his right leg, the result of long-standing circulation issues brought on by diabetes. A year later, the online news source Lede News reported that he remained a resident of Peterson. In his mid-60s

Moon Dog, Charles Waldrum, December 2012.

and dealing with the realization that his patrolling days were over, Charles Waldrum, like all of us, was in need of some encouragement and validation that his life had purpose.

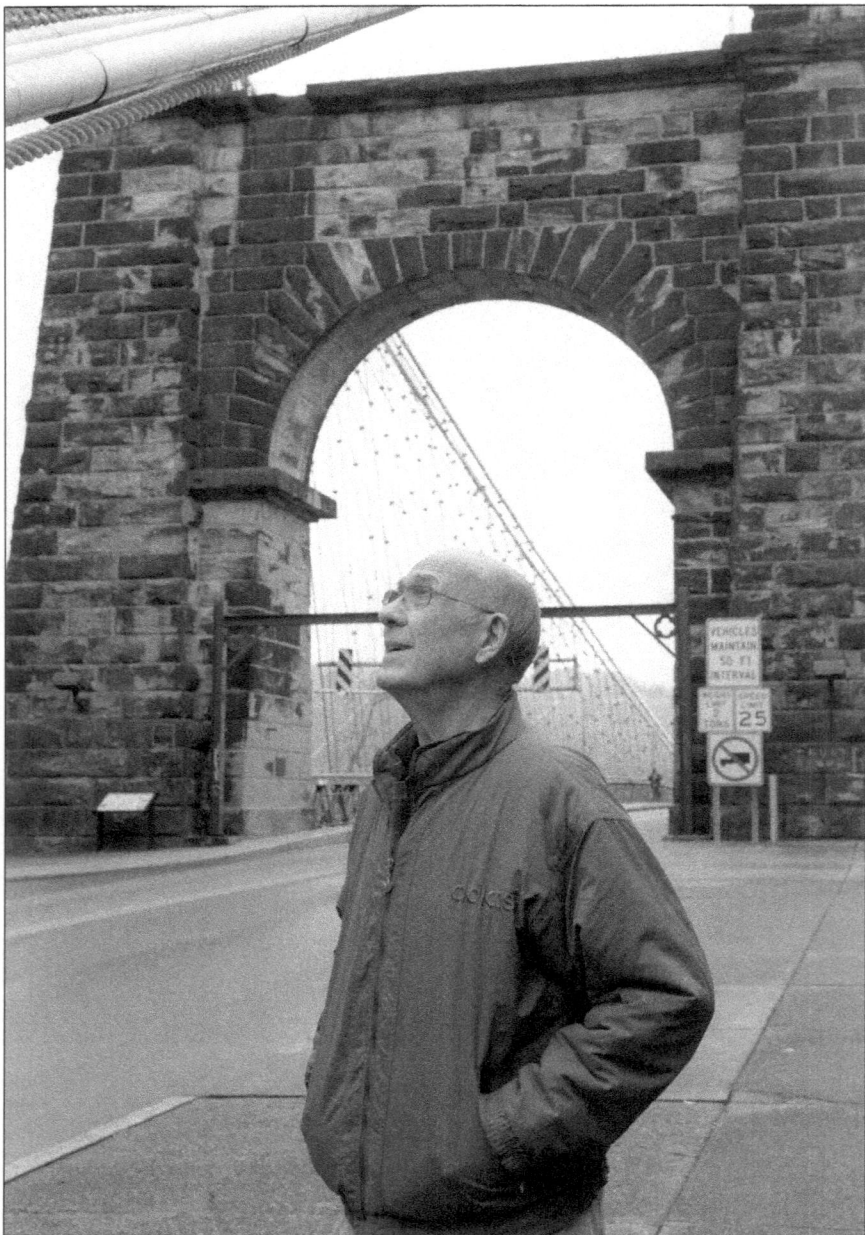

Dick Clark, the desk clerk at the Knights Inn of downtown Wheeling, was fascinated with the city's suspension bridge and its history.

Chapter 7

Suspended in Wheeling

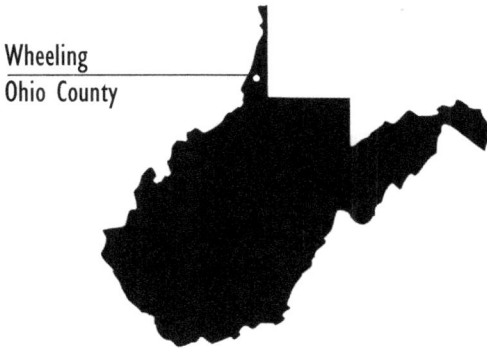

Wheeling
Ohio County

Dick Clark spoke about the Wheeling Suspension Bridge as if it were an old friend or neighbor, both of which were the case. "Dick's Bridge," as locals sometimes referred to the historic structure, had been standing for nearly 90 years when the London, Ohio, native was born.

I met Dick while working on the Moon Dog story in December 2012. Dick was the desk clerk/troubleshooter of the Main Street Knights Inn, an economical crash pad with a magnificent rooftop view of the historic bridge. The motel, often the site of drug activity and generally considered an eyesore "welcome-to-Wheeling" sign, has since been closed and purchased for re-development. The plan is to erect something that Wheeling and its residents can be proud of as visitors exit the Interstate and pass the historic bridge and prime-location lot. And, perhaps as Dick Clark did years ago, more folks will stop long enough to ponder the wonders of the bridge that links the city to Wheeling Island.

"I never paid any attention to that bridge until I came here," Dick told me as we sat in the hotel lobby. "I started to study the thing, and I had to ask, 'How did they do that?'"

The magnificent, historic Wheeling Suspension Bridge, as seen from the roof of the Knights Inn.

When the 1,040-foot suspension bridge opened in 1849, it was the longest of its kind in the world. Although the bridge held that distinction for only two years, Dick still marveled at this work of engineering, which carried the National Road's two lanes of traffic across the Ohio River. As Dick led me on a tour of the structure, he paused at the spot where the 12 steel cables that support the bridge descend into massive wooden enclosures near Main Street. Dick told me those cables continue under the streets for another two blocks before terminating in concrete.

The bridge was built in an era when the largest load would have been a horse and wagon, so only light passenger vehicles—4,000 pounds or less—were permitted in the modern era. Signs at each end warned drivers to maintain at least 50 feet between vehicles, and synchronized traffic lights at each portal were supposed to avoid overloading. To prevent tractor-trailer rigs, tour buses, and other large vehicles from using the bridge, height restraints were added between the stone arches. Dick witnessed

Dick Clark loved to talk about the Wheeling Suspension Bridge and the city in general with any person who checked into the motel or was just checking out the area around the bridge.

refrigerators, air conditioners, and televisions knocked off the roofs of vehicles whose drivers ignored the signage or didn't notice the bar.

Incredibly, motorists took their risks. On March 23, 2016, a Greyhound bus driver ignored the signs and collided with the restraint. The bridge was closed for inspection. Motorists' ongoing disregard for the bridge's limits finally forced its closure to vehicular traffic in September 2019. It remained open to pedestrians.

A stroll on the bridge, preferably on a day when the wind is calm, provides great views of the Ohio River, city, and the occasional string of barges. Dick encouraged motel guests to experience these wonders for themselves, he didn't warn them about the view that would be immediately below their feet.

"They get out on that bridge, and they can see right down through the deck to the river," he said. "I believe some of the women have been so mad at me when they got back that they would shoot me."

Dick also saw a few despondent people talked down from both the suspension bridge and parallel Interstate 70 bridge. He had little sympathy for people who were "so ignorant" to jump into the river from that height. The jumper would probably hit bottom before drowning, said Dick, who estimated the channel depth at 19 to 34 feet. "That's going to hurt. But if he is a swimmer, he'll do all right," Dick predicted.

In a more positive vein, Dick told stories of his years as an investor in the Riverboat Inn's bar, which serviced many of the stars who played at the city's legendary Capitol Music Hall. He was entrusted with a key to the backstage entrance and watched many shows from a special room near the stage. He recalled the weekend that Johnny Cash played the Capitol and seeing the $75,000 check that a music hall employee gave Cash at the end of the performance.

Dick also owned an accounting and computer business and was at that job when he had a call about a problem in the bar—two men were using offensive language. He approached them and told the men they had to clean up their language or take their conversation to the parking lot. They apologized, and Dick returned to his office.

That evening, Dick came back to the bar and found the two men still talking. The place was hopping with customers; his manager explained that the duo began paying for patrons' drinks shortly after Dick had reprimanded the men. A few days later, Dick received a letter from the men, apologizing for their behavior.

"Those two guys happened to be (country music stars) Dave Dudley and Faron Young," Dick said.

Chapter 8

A Tunnel, Twins & State Forest

Cabwaylingo State Forest
Wayne County

In southwestern West Virginia, four adjoining counties contribute por-
tions of their names to Cabwaylingo State Forest: CABell, WAYne,
LINcoln, and MinGO. Ironically, the state forest's 8,296 heavy forested
acres are entirely in Wayne County.

This bit of trivia came from Bonnie Watts, who was the forest office's
secretary for 34 years. I met her in May 2005 during a stay of several days
in the state forest, which dates to the 1930s and the Civilian Conservation
Corps.

Bonnie was born November 9, 1948, to Hubert and Ozalene Miller
Crum. Hubert was a twin brother to Hobert Crum. Bonnie, Hubert, and
Hobert are the main characters in our story and three of the nicest folks
I've ever met in West Virginia.

The boys were born May 29, 1923, to Flem and Evaline Johnson Crum.
Flem Crum was a farmer and excellent timber man who graded and sold
timber to earn the $1,200 needed to purchase his farm. He moved his
family there from their native Crum community in 1919.

A family farm was still an anomaly along the rail line in the 1920s.

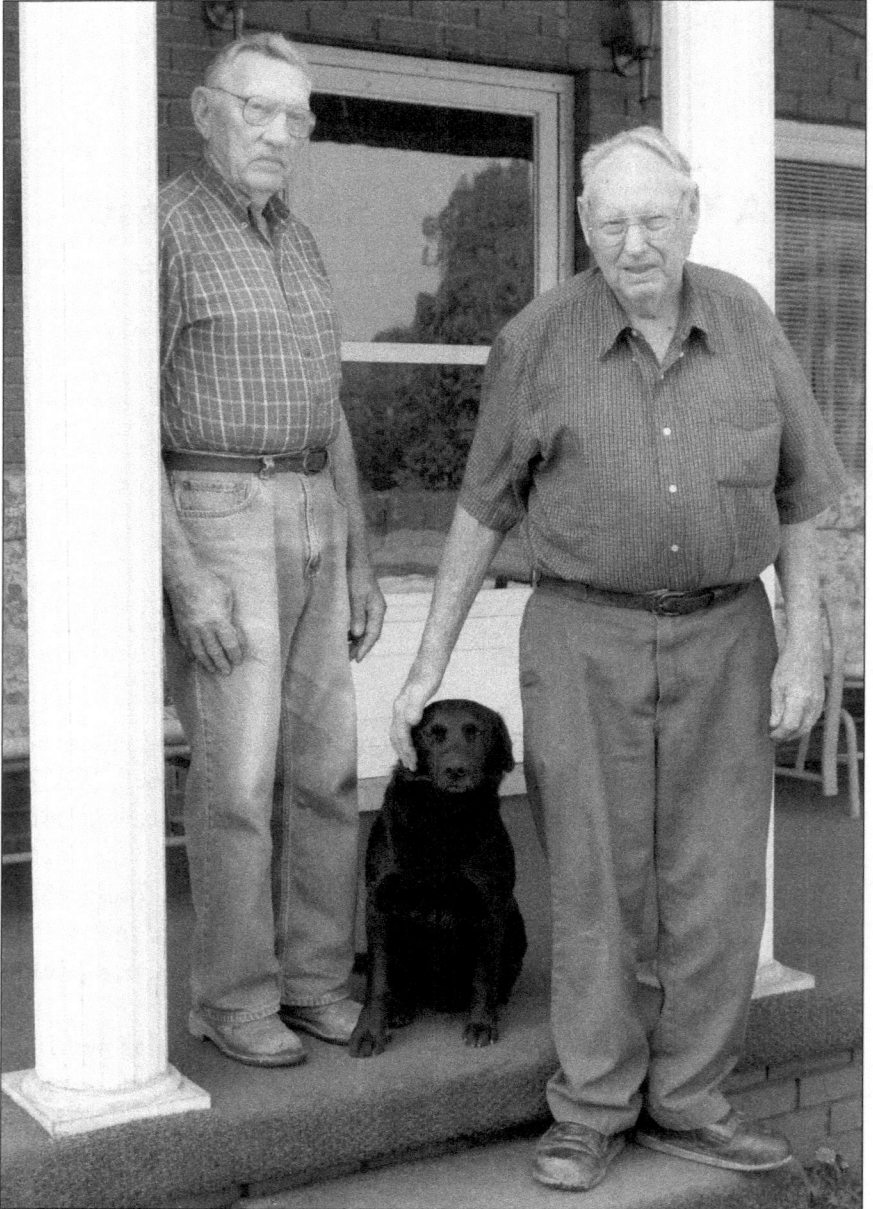

Hobert (left) and Hubert Crum pose with a pooch on the porch of Hobert's home in Cabwaylingo State Park. The twins were 83 when this image was made in May 2005.

The coal-mining boon that brought prosperity to McDowell and Mingo counties had not yet reached Wayne County although coal deposits existed there. Virgin forest, mainly stands of yellow popular, surrounded the Crum farmstead.

Most families lived along the ridges and eked out their livings with subsistence farming, timbering, and making moonshine, the region's most reliable cash crop. "You'd see smoke arisin' in every holler around here," Hobert told me as we sat on his front porch. The columns of smoke in the deep forests signaled hooch was being distilled.

Hobert's brother-in-law, Milton Mills, was a moonshiner. Hobert told me Milton went down to the train station one day to make a delivery, but the sheriff was waiting for him. The sheriff was certain Milton was there to conduct business, so he waited around to catch him in the act. Milton cleverly concealed the hooch underneath his bib overalls.

"The train come by, stopped, and Milton got on it and sold the whiskey to the engineer and conductor," Hobert said. The train continued up the line about a half-a-mile, then stopped so Milton could get off and evade the law.

Mingo County historian Herb Crum told me that moonshining paid better than most other occupations in this rugged region. "I interviewed an employee of the Yellow Poplar Lumber Company, and he said that he made $4 a day as a regular employee, but when he ran the moonshine still, he made $5 a day," Herb said. "Moonshine (consumption) seemed to be a part of the lifestyle of certain professions. Some people have been able to 'hold their liquor' and still continue their profession."

The arrival of outsiders via construction of the Norfolk and Western Railroad and Cabwaylingo State Forest infrastructure slowly ameliorated the Mingo County culture. But the county, which had been split off from Logan County in 1895, could not jettison its image and history. As home to the famous Hatfield clan, the county, to this day, remains connected to the feud between that clan and the McCoys, most of who lived across the river in Kentucky (McCoy patriarch Randolph McCoy was born in Logan County, Virginia). The feud, which began in 1882 and continued into the 1890s, eventually sent 13 persons to their early graves and spun one of Applachia's enduring stereotypes.

More violence and murder came to Mingo during the Mine Wars of

Matewan, 2005. The town and region make the most of their Hatfield-McCoy and massacre history.

the early 20th century. That bloodshed had a grand opening at Matewan, where the infamous shootout between Al Felts and Sid Hatfield occurred May 19, 1920. The latter was the town's police chief and supporter of the striking miners; the former worked for the Felts Detective Agency, which sent 13 detectives to Matewan to evict striking miners and their families from company houses. The confrontation at the Matewan railroad station left 10 persons dead—seven Baldwin Felts detectives, two miners, and the town's mayor. Sid Hatfield and the 17 strikers who were tried for murder walked away free men in early 1921. Later that year, Hatfield was gunned down at the McDowell County seat of Welch.

The reputation of "Bloody Mingo" was further entrenched in local lore when the Norfolk and Western Railroad arrived in the 1890s. Rich deposits of coal drew barons and the N&W to these parts. The industry exploded, along with racial discrimination fueled by an influence of workers immigrant and nonwhite workers. In 1892, the railroad expanded its reach with a line between Lenore and Wayne. This required a tunnel nearly a mile long that was dug through the mountain by Black laborers using only picks and shovels. Italian immigrants crafted the stonework on the tunnel's portal.

Dingess Tunnel before the only lights a motorist saw in there was the other end or headlights of an oncoming vehicle

The N&W bored the Dingess Tunnel as part of a 59-mile-long, single-track alignment, the Twelvepole Line, along the Big Sandy River between Naugatuk and the Ohio River at Credo. The road takes its name from Twelvepole Creek, which was found to be 12 poles (198 feet) wide at its mouth. Gristmills and sawmills were located along the stream, which also helped facilitate Wayne County's first industry, logging.

Opened to traffic in the early 1890s, the 3,311-foot-long Dingess Tunnel accommodated an eastbound track for empty coal car, local freight, and passenger traffic. Providing access to the region's rich bituminous coal resources of the region, the tunnel and railroad were responsible for both new towns and opportunities in the previously sparsely settled wilderness.

After Wayne County's coal deposits were discovered and exploited, a second track became necessary, and the tunnel soon became a victim of the success it spawned. The Big Sandy Alignment, completed in 1925, led to the abandonment of Twelvepole section between Lenore and Wayne eight years later. Eventually, the abandoned line was incorporated into a state highway and several county roads that include 33 bridges and two tunnels (the second one is considerably shorter than Dingess).

From its completion, the tunnel had value to the residents of Dingess as an access corridor to the outside world. Folks who used it as a pedestrian byway occasionally encountered a train and death in the dark recess. Several residents I spoke to said manholes were carved into the walls every few hundred feet in the event a pedestrian met an oncoming train or vehicle. Hubert Crum told me that murders hid in the holes and killed people as they passed through.

"They'd kill them and put (their bodies) back in the hole," he said.

"They" were supposedly railroad security workers who had an issue with hoboes and people of certain ethnic backgrounds riding the trains. Or they may have been bloodthirsty locals who saw the tunnel as the perfect place for committing a crime of hatred. These stories, whether legend, truth, or embellished, live on as part of Dingess Tunnel and Twelvepole Road lore.

Backwoods ways

Whatever the extent of the vices in this corner, it was the world in which Hobert and Hubert Crum were reared. Sitting on their porch with them that warm May morning in 2004, the landscape and moment were far removed from the murders and bloodshed of which they spoke. Eventually, the Bloody Mingo stories gave way to more personal stories of hardship.

The Norfolk Western line was the Crum family's main artery to the outside world. Travel to settlements like Dunlow and Crum was on foot or horseback. Hubert said that when their baby brother died at the age of nine months, their uncle carried the corpse on his lap while riding horseback to Crum, where the family buried the infant in the Crum Cemetery.

There was a dirt road that ran along the hill above their farm, but it was nothing more than a wagon path. Hobert said it was a common occurrence for his father to be called upon to hitch up his team of oxen and extract a vehicle mired in the mud and deep ruts of this crude byway. Wagons, sleds, and teams of horses were the common mode of transportation on it.

"Back then, there were just maybe one or two vehicles in this part of the country," Hubert said. "There was just one filling station around here, in Dunlow, and gas was 12 cents a gallon."

Day and night, coal trains labored on the rails that connected the vast coal resources of the Tug Fork River Valley to the outside world. Hobert

Hubert (left) and Hobart Crum collected and restored Model A cars. Each brother owned one of the Ford classics. May 2005.

said hobos frequently rode the coal trains in those days, and for some Black and foreign-born hobos, their trip through Wayne County was their last. Hubert recalled lawless members of the community expressing their prejudices by shooting the hobos as if they were game. "They were mean, uncivilized people back then," Hubert said.

Warning signs were placed along the line. "They said, 'N—, don't let the sun come down on you'" Hubert said. Those who could read and had the wisdom to heed the warning got off the train and took the next east-bound one out of the region. Trackmen who came upon a body usually buried it there without pursuing further investigation, the twins said.

Hobert said his father, who was justice of the peace for that district, was powerless in preventing or prosecuting these murders.

"Back in our days, you could kill somebody and skip over to Kentucky at Ten Mile and get away with it," Hobert said.

"They never knew what law was up here," Hubert said. "I never knew anybody to get (sent to prison) for killing someone."

Twelve Pole Creek, at a spot where it is far from 12 poles wide.

Even blood itself could not stop the bloodshed. The twins recalled a gun battle between feuding families that resulted in a mule or horse being shot out from underneath a Ferguson man. The injured man was left on a railroad bridge for a train's engineer to discover.

"On that bridge, he laid there until he died," Hobert said.

The Civil War continued to be fought in their settlement, as well. John Lowe, who had served in the Confederate Army, lived on the property that Hobert came to own. Two other Civil War veterans, "Uncle" Joe and Isaac Marcum, also lived in the community. Joe had been a Rebel, Isaac a Union soldier. Quarrels between the two veterans were ongoing, and despite threatening physical harm to each other, the men were too feeble to make good on them.

Herb Dawson, a regional historian, questioned the magnitude of the twins' version of hobo and sniper killings, however.

"In reading of the newspapers of 1900 through 1950, there are very few references of people being killed as they rode the train as hoboes," he told me. "There are references to hobos being killed or being found dead in the

Kenova or Williamson yards. These definitely tend to be isolated cases. It was not an everyday occasion. The railroad depots were a gathering place. This would have been where the action happened because of the traffic that the trains created."

It was against this backdrop of violence, isolation, and ignorance that the state forest designation and its recreational development came into existence. Conversion of the former N&W rail bed to a highway was a catalyst for this project as it opened the region to vehicular traffic.

The twins recalled area men working on the project, which came under the Works Progress Administration (WPA). Men from the area who previously spent their days moonshining found another, albeit more difficult, way to earn cash by building a roadbed of rock 12 inches thick.

A train that worked ahead of the highway work zone transported the rails and ties out of the region. Rails were loaded onto flat cars as quickly as the crews could dislodge and hoist them. "They man-handled all that stuff," Herb said. "They'd have eight to 10 men pick up one of them big rails and put it on a flat car."

Building Cabwaylingo

Hobert said the Bill Floyd Land Company purchased as many acres in the area as possible to create a single tract of forest. Most of the purchases were of small farms, but their father refused to sell his land. To this day, there are numerous private tracts within the state forest, Flem's included.

Once the land company had acquired 6,196 acres, it sold the total tract to the state for $2 an acre. Over the years, additional purchases increased the holding to 8,296 acres.

Two Civilian Conservation Corps (CCC) camps were established. Camp Anthony Wayne opened July 4, 1935, within the state forest. It closed April 11, 1939. The CCC barracks for this camp would later become the group camp.

Camp Twelve-Pole opened just across the Wayne County line in Mingo County at the mouth of Poor Branch of Twelvepole Creek. It was established July 13, 1935, and closed on April 5, 1937. Camp Twelve-Pole's workers were assigned to fire control, forest stand improvement, recreation

The Civilian Conservation Corps built Cabwaylingo's beautiful structures.

development, wildlife feeding, surveys, and stream improvement to benefit the forest.

Camp Anthony Wayne's workers built the massive stone and timber cabins, shelters, steps, and other park amenities. Hope returned to the region.

"It was exciting to us," Hobert said. "There was nothing like that around here until they came in."

The twins were too young to work on the CCC projects when they were built in 1935 and '36. But they remember the positive impact the camps and outside investment had on the area. They say the CCC workers interacted with residents and some of the young men ended up marrying local girls. Some stayed behind and found careers with the state or coal and timber operations.

Bonnie Crum Watts made a career of Cabwaylingo and, as its secretary, was the human face many visitors came to associate with the forest. She was hired by the state under the Comprehensive Employment and Training Act (CETA) June 21, 1976, and worked for the forest longer than any other employee in its history.

"Bonnie is Cabwaylingo State Forest," Clisby Jennelle, IV, park

Bonnie Crum Watts grew up within the forest boundaries and found her dream
job at Cabwaylingo.

superintendent told me in 2005. "There are a lot of people who will call
in, and if Bonnie doesn't answer the phone and I happen to pick it up, will
say 'That's all right, we'd rather talk to Bonnie, we'll call back.'"

By Bonnie's accounting, Clisby was the 11th superintendent she had
worked for since starting her job. She also worked under at least nine other
state supervisory personnel who pulled interim duty at Cabwaylingo.

Bonnie had the good fortune of growing up with this forest as her
playground. Even the first several months of her elementary education, in
the fall and early winter of 1954, were spent in Cabwaylingo.

"It was only a one-room (school) with grades one through eight," she
recalled. "All students attended classes at the same time. Each class had its
own designated area within that one room, and there was one teacher for
the students. Her name was Anna Kirk."

The schoolhouse was in Doane Hollow, directly across the road from
the park's swimming pool. Long before there was a pool here, Halcey
Maynard operated a grocery store with gasoline pumps on what was a
private tract of land.

The trails at Cabwaylingo were constructed by members of the Civilian Conservation Corps during the 1930s. Decades later, these trails still provide access to nature and solitude in the state forest.

After the new elementary school opened at Dunlow, the little schoolhouse in the woodland was razed. But the forest remained a popular destination for school outings. "We were allowed one day per year for field day," she said. "We'd have it at the Long Branch picnic area. We would play horseshoe and ball; have a cookout. The school would provide lunch. We would ride the bus there and then back to school when it was time to go home. We always had it in the spring, right before school ended."

Growing up with parents who made family time a priority, Bonnie spent a portion of every Sunday in the park picnicking, playing a ball game with neighbor kids, and enjoying the natural beauty of the forest and streams.

Of all her childhood memories of the park, none looms larger than that of the family reunions held there the second Sunday in September. Although it was called the Perry-Maynard Reunion, people from all over the area turned out for the event, which evolved into the Maynard Reunion. But

Bonnie Watts recalled the huge family reunions held at the Long Branch picnic area at Cabwaylingo.

in Bonnie's childhood years, the reunion drew between 2,000 and 2,500 persons. Bonnie said vehicles parked on both sides of the road for several miles as folks gathered in the forest.

Held in the Long Branch picnic pavilion, the reunion sprawled over the grounds and onto the surrounding hillsides. "The tables would be lined with home-cooked picnic dishes made by the women," Bonnie recalled. "There were games, singing, contests, speeches, and a wonderful time had by all. This was the largest one-day gathering in the forest."

The caliber of entertainment at these reunions was in keeping with their magnitude. Bonnie recalls hearing performances by Earl Flatt and Lester Scruggs, Minnie Pearl, and String Bean. With so many constituents gathered in one place, the reunion was a popular destination for politicians. "Governor Arch Moore flew in on his helicopter to attend," she said. "They landed it across the road from the Long Branch Picnic area."

Stone picnic shelters built by the Civilian Conservation Corps have stood the test of time and elements at Cabwaylingo.

Despite these pleasant childhood experiences, Bonnie set her sights on the big city when she graduated from Crum High School in 1966. "Growing up, it never once ran through my mind that I would ever work at Cabwaylingo," she said. "As a country child growing up, my dream was to get out of the country and get into the big city."

For Bonnie, that big city was Huntington, 45 miles to the north. Bonnie attended Huntington Business College, where she majored in accounting. Within two years of graduating, she married Ronnie Watts, a Wayne County native.

For five years, Bonnie worked in Huntington as a seamstress for the Sunset Furniture Company. Her husband worked there as an upholsterer. After their first child, Ronnie II, was born in 1973, their attitude toward city life changed. Bonnie said they wanted to raise their son in the rural atmosphere they'd known as children. They moved back to Wayne County and purchased a mobile home. Ronnie started working with Bonnie's father, who was in the construction business.

"The guy I worked for at Sunset made a trip all the way out here and begged me to come back to work for him," said Bonnie, who put her upholstery skills to work in her father's and uncle's antique cars.

She learned about the Cabwaylingo opportunity from Wilma Jarrell, the wife of Lacy Jarrell, park superintendent for 23 years. She was hired as the secretary's assistant, responsible for answering the phone, making cabin reservations, and handling other office duties. Bonnie worked under the CETA program for three years before she became a state employee and was given the title of secretary. The thing that stands out in Bonnie's mind about those early years was the incidence of forest fires.

"We've had some major fires here. This was really a hot area," she said. "When I first came to work here, there would be as high as 10 men sacked out in my backroom. They'd stay all night and stay two or three nights if we were having a bad fire season."

The Tick Ridge fire tower, built in 1935, was still in use (it is still standing but not accessible). Crews composed of paid fire wardens and local men wielding nothing more than hand tools battled the blazes. Forestry Division men who fought fires in Cabwaylingo included Gerald Wimer, Coy Mullins, John Looney, Bob Beanblossom, Jim Dickerson, Joe Lucas, Tex Fields, and Larry Six, Bonnie recalled.

"They had to stay in the forest many nights to help save the timber and its natural resources," said Bonnie.

Bonnie also recalled how the forest suffered from another manifestation of nature's fury in 1977 and 1978. Extensive flooding along the Tug Fork and its tributaries forced many residents from their homes and into the park for shelter. "Almost each person in the Dunlow and surrounding areas was affected," recalled Bonnie. "Many lost everything they owned and had to start all over."

Many of these flood victims were housed in cabins until services were restored.

"We had community residents sleeping in the forest headquarters/office building until they could be relocated," Bonnie said. The C&P Telephone Company set up shop in the park's group camp facility and workers were

The park superintendent's home was built by the Civilian Conservation Corps.

housed there until service was restored to the Dunlow, Moses Fork, and Crum areas—about three months.

Bonnie's office also served as the first-aid station, and over the years she's patched up her share of scratches, scrapes, and burns. Amazingly, she's never had to treat a snake bite—Bonnie said Cabwaylingo has a reputation for its copperhead population, although encounters have decreased from when she first started there.

"When they were building the Tick Ridge Campground, it wasn't unusual for the men to come in at the end of the day and report killing 25 to 30 copperheads," she said. "It was nothing for them to find 20 to 30 copperheads in a day."

Most guests had their sole encounter with a poisonous snake in Bonnie's office. Coiled up under glass on the counter was a very dead baby rattlesnake, a gift from a local resident.

Visitors occasionally encountered a snake in their cabins, however. As temperatures dropped in the fall, the warmth-seeking snakes entered the structures. "City people, it would frighten them to death, they'd be really, really scared," Bonnie said of guests who dashed into the office (there were no landline phones in the cabins) after finding an intruder in their cabin.

Bonnie acknowledged that for some "city people," Cabwaylingo was just too remote and rustic. When a first-time park user called to make a reservation, Bonnie alerted them to the park's spartan realities. "I'll ask them what type of activities they are looking for, and if they say they want horseback riding, golf, and things like that, then I will recommend one of the other parks," she said. Shopping? Forget it unless you want to drive for at least an hour.

Cabwaylingo is best suited for the family that enjoys the simple things in life. Opportunities include hunting on the state forestland during respective state hunting seasons and fishing in Twelvepole Creek, which is stocked with trout in early spring. There are 25 miles of nature trails and two waterfalls, one of which rivals Blackwater in height. Overhanging rock cliffs are along several of the trails.

"If you like nature, you'll love it here," she said. "If you like bird watching, doing simple things, then you'll like it. A lot of people come here looking for an elaborate Holiday Inn type of thing. They end up not liking it because it is so far out in the country and they don't like the rustic feel of it. It's very remote and mountainous here."

Hobert Crum died April 15, 2020, at the age of 96. Hubert preceded him in death September 23, 2006, a year after our conversation on the front porch of Hobert's home. Bonnie Watts, the face of Cabwaylingo State Forest, died August 3, 2019.

The park she and her family loved so dearly remains with its CCC-era structures, vast woodlands, streams, 19 cabins, copperheads, and Tug River Valley lore. It is home to the Cabwaylingo Trail, the first in the Hatfield-McCoy Trail System to be located within a West Virginia state forest. The trail is dedicated to ATV, UTV, 4x4, and dirt bike recreation.

Return to Dingess Tunnel

As for the Dingess Tunnel, much has improved since my passage through it in 2005. At that time, the tunnel had no artificial lighting in its interior. A driver had to check for the headlamps of oncoming traffic before entering it and hope any motorist entering at the other end did the same. Going forward through the skinny tunnel was scary enough; I can't image what backing out would have been like.

Dingess Tunnel on the inside looking out, a welcome return to daylight.

I was driving a Mazda 5 with a moon roof and manual transmission the day we went through. The contrast between the sunny morning and the dark cave was startling. The noise of the engine revving and echoing through the rock enclosure was as deafening as the darkness was startling. The open moon roof made the roar worse, and we soon realized it also allowed water dripping from the tunnel's ceiling to enter our cabin.

Standing near the entrance and listening to the approach of a vehicle from the opposite end was another unworldly experience. The sound started as a low roar that grew to a deafening level as the tiny dots of light slowly grew larger. Based upon the noise level, you would expect to see 18-wheel behemoth emerge, not a compact car.

Vehicles plowing through this space generated a stiff wind that could be felt at the portals. One local told me that a train passing through the tunnel created a vacuum so strong it would suck a pedestrian right under its wheels. That makes me wonder just how beneficial those manholes would have been for someone trapped in the tunnel. Further, concerning those hobo bodies discovered in its icy darkness, I wonder if those victims were murdered or suffered a heart attack when they realized they were about to meet their maker in the Dingess Tunnel.

When signs like this one fail, trouble is not far behind.

I nearly suffered a cardiac event myself the morning I visited the tunnel. I'd heard that Blaze Starr (1932-2015), the famous stripper from West Virginia, lived near the tunnel at Wilsondale. I did my research by making an inquiry at the house above Dingess Tunnel. Naively, I took the back route up the incline, navigating weeds and brush, scared to death of encountering a copperhead or unfriendly landowner adept in nailing a trespasser with a single shot.

It was a fruitless endeavor. I never found Blaze Starr's house, which was probably just as well—the *GOLDENSEAL* editor likely would have censored it. But I always thought "The Hottest Blaze in Burlesque," aka Fanny Belle Fleming from Wayne County, would have made a great interview and story. And,I was not alone in that search. Bonnie Watts told me one of the most frequent inquiries she received at the state forest office was, "Can you tell me where the stripper lives?"

Incidentally, for those interested in exploring family history in that region, a cemetery, Tunnel Hill, is on the land over the tunnel, which bears the surname of the folks buried there: W.A., Jesse, Lloyd, Vina, Ray, Emma Jean, and Dorothy Dingess.

Twenty years later, I hanker to go back to Dingess Tunnel and see the

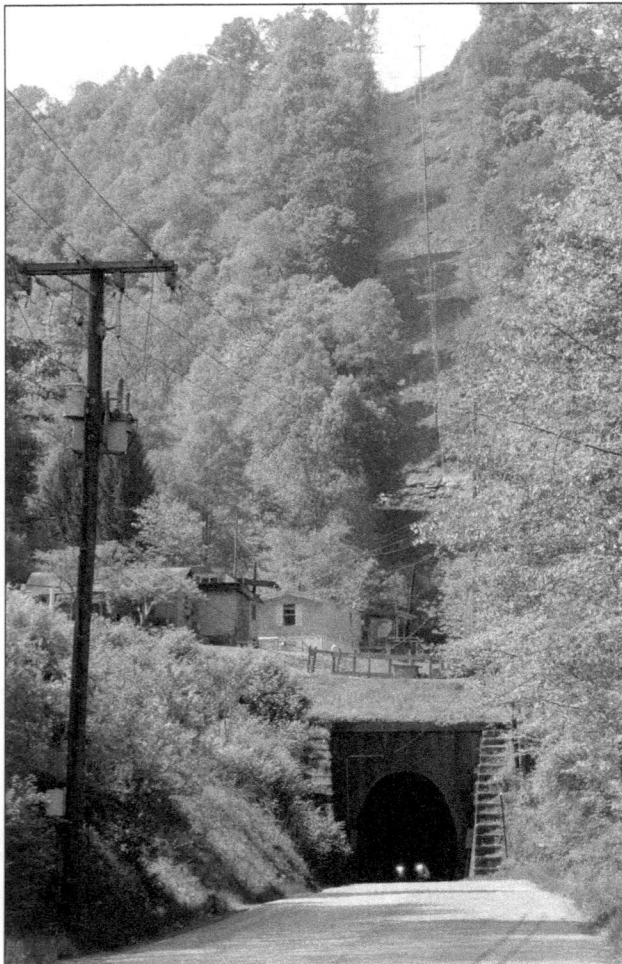

The steep hill explains why it was easier to build a tunnel than move a mountain. One of the legends birthed by the tunnel states that the first locomotive to attempt passage through the it got stuck in there and the crew members were asphyxiated.

improvements made during a $5.5 million project that included LED lighting, replacing the steel liner, adding new drains, and repaving the roadway.

Then again, perhaps such places are best remembered for how they were rather than what they've become. Further, several rough times in my life since that visit have mirrored the experience of traversing Dingess Tunnel in a subcompact with a moon roof—only a pinpoint of light to guide me, no option to back out, troubles dripping from the ceiling, the noise of anxiety deafening. How glorious and welcome was that sunlight when I finally emerged and resumed my wanderings!

Along the way: God and politics

onventional wisdom warns against mixing religion with politics, especially at family gatherings and in the presence of alcohol. In West Virginia, however, politics and faith often co-exist on barns, trees, and even the entrance to the Dingess Tunnel. Here are three examples of these interesting and sometimes humorous juxtapositions.

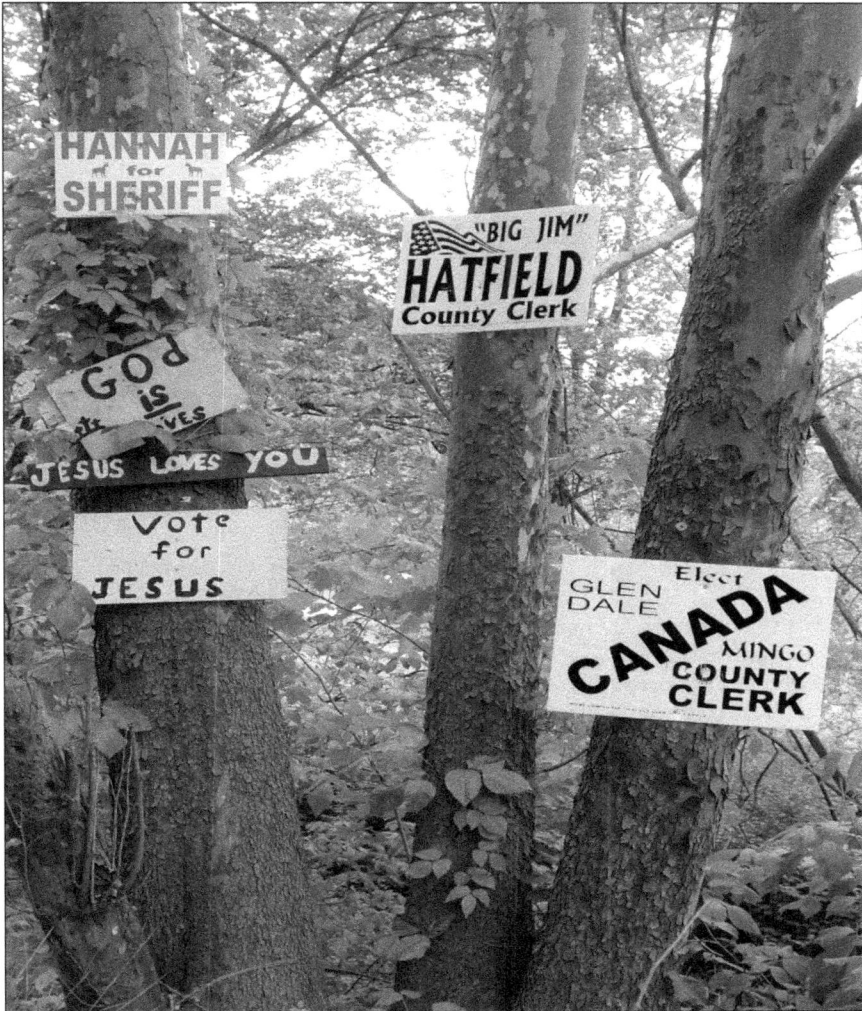

Mingo County political signs. It must have been an interesting ballot that year.

Motorists fearful of what horrors lurked in the Dingess Tunnel in 2004 were encouraged to "Try God" by a graffiti artist who defaced the lovely 1914 stonework at the tunnel's entrances. Politicians placed their messages above the tunnel portal, presumably to distract drivers from oncoming headlights. I think the persons with the most faith in the above image were the truck driver and whoever was entering the tunnel at the other end.

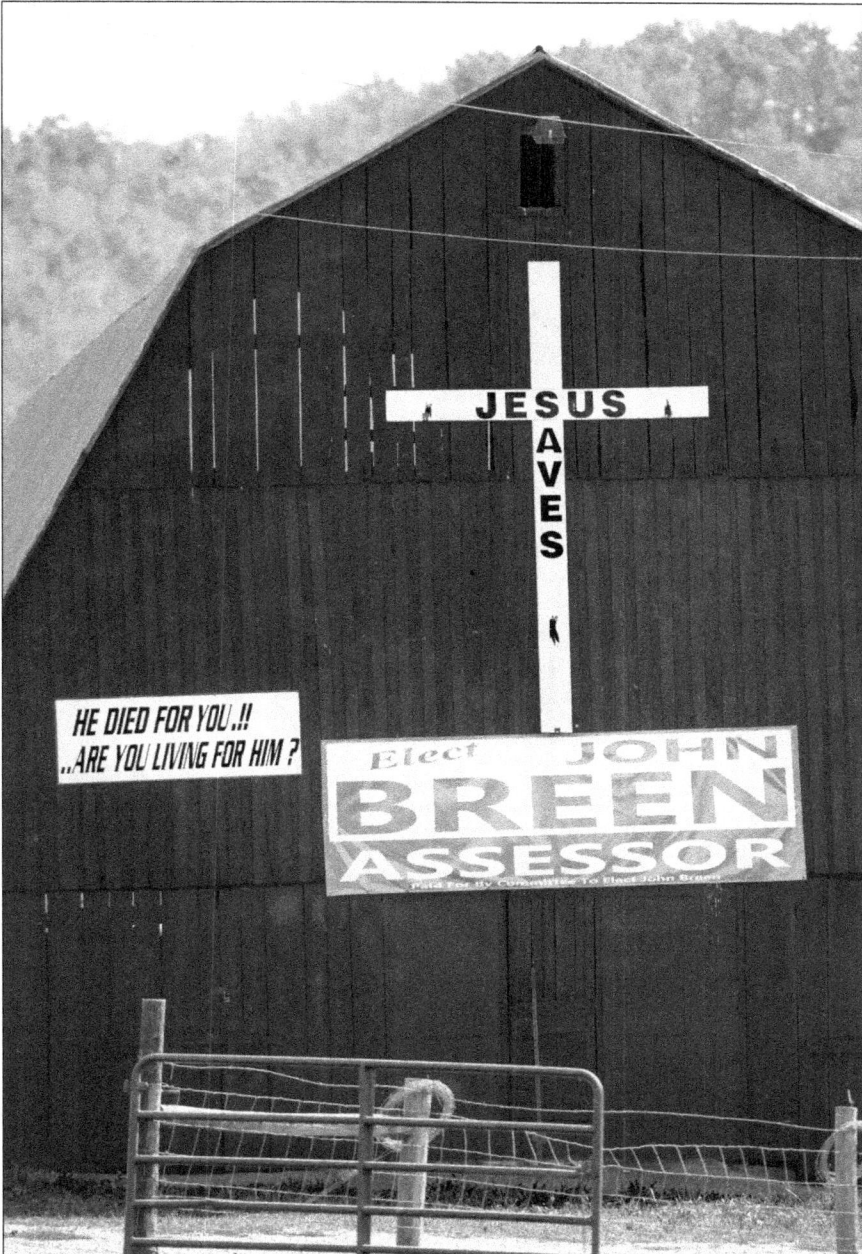

I wonder if candidate John Breen approved this juxtaposition on a Lewis County barn?

Reno Calemine at work in his shoe repair shop, October 2016. He was 90 years old and still riding his bicycle to work several days a week.

Chapter 9

Saving Soles in Keyser

Keyser
Mineral County

The last time I visited 25 Armstrong Street, Keyser, the storefront was vacant. But in the window was a memorial to Guerino Josrph "Reno" Calemine, who for decades practiced the cobbler's craft at Calemine's Patriotic Shoe Shop. The memorial might still be there for all I know. This much is certain: Any retailer or service provider who took up residence there had big shoes to fill.

Reno departed his shoes and mortality February 23, 2017, three months after I spent an afternoon with him in the shop that his father, Domenico Cosimo "Domenick" Calemine, founded in 1914.

"He came here when he was 16 years old," Reno said of his father, who immigrated from Caulonia, Calabria, Italy. "He came by himself. He landed in Rome, New York, where he paid $5 to get a job. He worked a week, then was let go. That's the way they treated immigrants back then," Reno said.

While working in a Youngstown, Ohio, nail factory, Domenick received word from a cousin, John Fanto, that he could get him a job on the Baltimore and Ohio Railroad at Piedmont, West Virginia.

"He got a job on the work train, and that's how he ended up in Piedmont," Reno said of the town near Keyser.

When they were not maintaining or building railroads, the workers played poker in a caboose. "Another train came along and collided with their caboose. Two people got killed, and my father's legs were smashed, all broken," Reno said.

At the Keyser hospital where the injured were treated, a Dr. Hoffman insisted that Domenick's mangled leg be amputated. Domenick, unable to speak English, adamantly expressed through an interpreter that he would be extremely "disappointed" if that happened. After several impassioned exchanges about the leg, the doctor agreed to wire together the shattered pieces and thereby save the limb.

"And you know, I saw an X-ray of that leg when my father was 80 years old, and you could see the wire still in there," Reno said.

His father spent a year in the hospital, and the B&O covered the cost. A nurse, "Mrs. Romig," taught him how to speak and read English during his recuperation. No longer capable of doing the hard labor of railroad employment, Domenick opened a cobbler shop.

Reno said his father learned the trade while living in Italy. Keyser already had several shoe repair shops, but there was enough business to support one more, thanks to its railroad-town status. His father set up shop in a frame building on Armstrong Street. The little shop, run by an immigrant with a limp, prospered.

"In 1913, he went back to Italy. Apparently, he had made enough money that he could afford to close this place (for a while) and go back. While he was there, he met his wife, Teresa Calemine (1896-1982). No relation to each other," Reno said.

Domenick brought his bride to the United States and settled in Keyser. "He liked Keyser, and this is where he wanted to stay," Reno said. "My father and mother are both buried here."

When America sent its young men into the battlefields of World War I, Domenick tried to enlist, but he was rejected. Domenick did his part by being the most patriotic person in Keyser. He played the part of Uncle Sam in minstrel shows and parades; he sold Liberty Bonds at his shop.

"He sold more Liberty Bonds than anybody else around here," Reno

Guerino "Reno" Calemine laughs about a comment made by one of the visitors to his shop. October 2016.

said. "One day he came to work, and the sign was on his shoe shop: 'Calemine's Patriotic Shoe Shop.'"

The name stuck, as did the Calemine family's patriotic streak. The couple had four boys and each one served his nation. First-born Carlo was at Pearl Harbor when the Japanese attack came. He served in the Army Air Force throughout World War II and received several Purple Hearts. "He had shrapnel in his head, and they buried him with that in there," Reno said of Carlo, who lived to be 89. He chose a career path other than shoe repair.

Orlando, the second born, went into shoe repair in North Carolina. He died at 68.

Reno, born March 5, 1926, was next in line. He entered the armed forces when he turned 18 in 1945. He was assigned to Camp Lee, Virginia, in the shoe repair section. Reno explained that a large number of World War II veterans who had suffered orthopedic injuries required custom footwear. A sergeant who taught in the orthopedics section gave Reno access to

Guerino "Reno" Calemine demonstrates the use of a machine that nails the soles onto the upper section of the shoe. October 2016.

the lab. "He let me fool around in there, and that's where I really picked up the skills to take care of wounded soldiers," Reno said.

Julio was the last child born to the couple.

"He was in the shoe repair business, too. He went into it in the Cumberland (Maryland) area. He retired (circa 2007) and he wished he had not. He told me, 'Retirement is not the best thing when you are our age. All you do is sit and sit. And pretty soon, you can't walk,'" Reno said.

Reno heeded his brother's advice and refused to suffer the same fate. "I'm here because I didn't want to stay home," he declared. "My wife pays me $50 a month to come over here." When pressed for the truth, Reno confessed that the stipend from his wife, Elva, was one of the many stories that floated around the shop.

Working late into life is all about self-preservation, he said.

"I want to stay mobile until I die," he said. "If I keep working, I'll be that

Domenick Calemine and his son Guerino "Reno" are shown in this snapshot from 1963. Domenick died October 10, 1970. *Calemine family collection.*

way; that's the trick. Whoever says that retirement is the golden years is crazy. Those people who retire and sit down, (they) end up in the nursing home. Retirement is not the golden years unless you keep yourself busy. The truth is the golden years are those years leading up to retirement."

"There ain't no disgrace to growing old. It's just inconvenient," Reno added.

Putting a shine on life

His shop was open Monday, Tuesday, Thursday, and Friday, 10 a.m. to 4 p.m. If Reno had a doctor's appointment or other personal obligation, he called on a friend, Greg Rotrock, to open the shop, assist customers, and accommodate the gang that claimed the shop as its clubhouse.

Reno Calemine pedaled his bicycle to work most days. He also grew a large vegetable garden for himself, neighbors and customers, of his Armstrong Street shoe shop.

"He has the key to this place, and when I can't come over, I give him a ring. I've always kept this place open so (his friends who loiter in the shop) have a place to go," Reno said. "I usually have company from the time I am open. If I am busy, I don't pay any attention to them and go back and work."

Reno and his comrades, known as the "B.S. College," socialized in the front area of the 14-foot-wide shop. They sat on four kitchen chairs perched on the shoe-shine platform that came from a Main Street hotel in Keyser. The marble platform had stanchions of pure brass and was as much a fixture in the place as the Calemine family.

"This was a five-seater," Reno said. "But this place is too small for five seats, so (his father) cut it down to four."

While the shoe-shine station closed for business years ago, it once was the shop's most popular service. Reno said there were several dance halls in the Keyser area during the first half of the 20th century, and no dapper gentleman would dare enter one without a shine on his shoes. Dominick, and later Reno, hired young men to shine shoes for this clientele after the shop closed on Saturdays. Many of those men who worked for Reno reminisced about that era decades later. "Jimmy, Gerald, Bubb ," Reno said, naming a few of the bootblacks who worked for the Calemines.

"The place would be open until 9 or 10 p.m.," Reno said. "There were five shoe shops in Keyser in those days, and there were three more in Piedmont."

A basic black shoe shine cost a nickel, a white shine a dime, and tan shoes were 15 cents when Reno began polishing them at the age of 8. "This is where I learned the shoe repair business," Reno said, motioning to the row of seats. "I bought my first bicycle with money from shining shoes." The bicycle cost $24.00. Reno also purchased all his clothes with his shoe shine money; his father allowed him to keep everything he made, but he reimbursed his father for the polish.

"Ever since I started shining shoes, I never asked Dad for money," Reno said.

Reno received free vocational education as part of the deal. The first task he learned in the workroom was removing the soles from shoes.

"Step by step, that's how I learned," he said. For more than 80 years, cobbler work was the only job he ever had.

"There was never a better boss," Reno said of his father, who instilled work ethic alongside the skills of the trade.

"If it took me all day to put on a pair of heels, that was OK. He wanted it done right," Reno said. "'Speed comes after perfection,' he used to tell me. 'I want you to do the job right.' And he always said, 'The customer is always right. Right or wrong, he or she is always right.' We tried to do everything right."

Reno and Elva raised two children, and while their son, also named Guerino was trained in the shop, he chose a career in food service. Their daughter, Carla Hastings, stayed in Keyser.

Reno eventually found himself a savior of soles in a world of disposable shoes. Ironically, through his tenacity and refusal to retire, Reno's services were in demand. Even in metropolitan areas like Washington, D.C., finding a cobbler can be difficult.

Reno relaxes in a kitchen chair perched on what was once a shoe shine station from a Keyser hotel. Calemine's was a gathering point for members of the local "BS Club." Greg Rotrock sits next to him. October 2016.

One of Reno's customers, David White, drove 110 miles from Ashburn, Virginia, to have new soles put on his dress shoes. Even factoring in the cost of driving 440 miles, White considered it a bargain.

"For $27 I got a new pair of shoes," said the U.S. Coast Guard/Navy commander retired, who grew up in Keyser. Reno said that job probably would have cost two to three times as much in a metropolitan shop.

With fewer than 10,000 feet in Keyser, the county seat of Mineral County, Reno depended upon customers from outside the community. His shelves of completed work were filled with shoes, boots, and purses from out-of-town, out-of-state, and occasionally foreign customers who found the shop by word of mouth.

"If I were to advertise, I would be so doggone busy," Reno said. "But I'm doing fine this way."

Reno claimed that most of what he made in the shop went for overhead: taxes, insurance, utilities, and rent—he didn't own the little building at 25 Armstrong Street. Originally, the shop was in a wood structure at that address. A fire consumed the building and threatened to claim his father's

Guerino "Reno" Calemine takes a break in his workroom next to one of the antique sewing machines in the shop. October 2016.

tools, as well. Neighbors and strangers alike rushed into the burning building to rescue the family's precious equipment and tools.

"I was so surprised at how all these people came out to save the shoe shop," Reno said.

The equipment suffered smoke and water damage but was salvaged and stored in a building across the street. The next day, Reno and Dominick received an offer from the bank where Reno had recently signed for a $6,500 loan to finish building a house for his family. At first, he was worried the loan officer would renege on the loan commitment after learning about the fire. Instead, the bank offered the Calemines a temporary home for their business in a former whiskey store property where bank records were stored. It was a huge place. "I said, 'Are you crazy? I got enough to pay for without that big place,'" Reno said. But the bank was more interested in keeping a cobbler's shop open than being paid a fair rent. For the next six months, while a new block building was built on the old site, Calemine's Patriotic Shoe Shop did business next to the bank.

"I had a (cobbler-supplies) salesman come in and tell me that I had the biggest shoe repair shop in the world!" Reno said.

Nearly 70 years later, Reno still ran his business with the vintage tools and equipment that Keyser's citizens salvaged from the fire. Reno said the reason that he could keep his prices low was because the business was free of debt. And Reno took care of his equipment; it had to last him the rest of his life.

"It is OK if I die over here because that will mean that I died on my two feet," Reno told me as we wrapped up the interview. "As long as I can come over here and work, I am going to do that."

In what may be one of the finest obituaries ever published in a West Virginia newspaper, Guerino Calemine was honored as a cobbler who "saved countless soles," "set the standard for being a model husband and father," and headed up what was Mineral County's oldest business. He still found time to raise a huge vegetable garden to feed family and friends, serve on the Keyser Town Council and as a water commissioner, and ride a bicycle to work until a few weeks before his passing.

"He hated sitting still," the obituary noted.

Chapter 10

Miracle in Coalwood

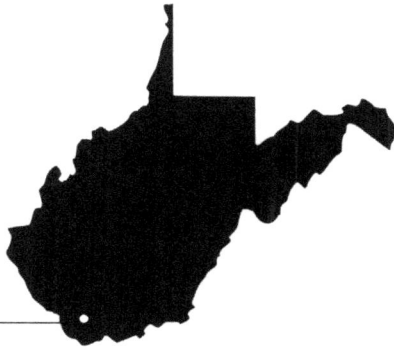

Coalwood
McDowell County

If you wandered into the McDowell County town of Coalwood on a spring morning in 2004, you would have encountered Dave Cross III waving to traffic at the intersection of Highway 16 and Main Street Row. And, if you'd gone into Country Corner, the town's only gas station and convenience store, you might have bumped into Ernest O'Dell (Red) Carroll as he visited with other Coalwood old-timers.

The O'Carroll name would ring a bell with you had you read Homer "Sonny" Hickam Jr.'s books or seen the 1999 Hollywood movie, *October Sky,* which was based on Hickam's 1998 best seller, *Rocket Boys.* Red's son was Jimmy O'Dell Carroll, one of the young scientists who helped put Coalwood in the history books.

Compelled by the NASA engineer's books and the movie, visitors from at least eleven foreign nations and all fifty states have come to Coalwood to see the fabled community firsthand. The two-lane, paved State Highway 16 leads to Coalwood off Route 52, just west of Welch. The curvy road struggles against Welch Mountain for five miles before giving way to the town of Coalwood, identified by a large, hand-painted sign at the "T" intersection. The boyhood home of Homer Hickam, a private residence, stands at this intersection. Route 16 continues to the left, passing the now vacant land where Olga Coal's Number One tipple once stood, and leads to the town of War, where Hickam went to high school. Frog Level Road, the main drag through Coalwood, is to the right. A couple of miles down this road, just past the white Pentecostal church and at the end of Jimmy O'Dell Street, was where Red and his wife, Ivy, lived.

Red was the man you wanted to see for a tour of Coalwood. If you expressed your interest at Country Corner, the clerk would ring his house and summon Red. Unless he was extremely busy with his garden, beehives, chickens, or dahlias, Red would drive his worn pickup to the corner and guide you through the town.

Tall and thin, his steps quick and body nimble, Red was in his late 80s when I met him that morning in June 2004. The red hair that became his namesake had disappeared, but beneath the Mack truck ball cap that kept the sun from burning his scalp was a mind full of memories and facts about the Coalwood of Homer Hickam's era.

He had lived in Coalwood his entire life and seen both the best and worst of times there. From his perspective, the worst years were during the Great Depression; no work was to be had. The best years were during World War II, when Consolidation Coal's mines were operating at full capacity. Red never worked underground, but from 1938 to 1954 he was employed on the tipple that loaded coal into the railroad cars.

The last surviving father of a Rocket Boy, Red was Coalwood's ambassador, and a very busy one at that. In just one week of August 2003, he led 427 visitors on his personalized tour of Coalwood.

He knew each one of the 877 homes in Coalwood from his work as the town's trash collector from 1954 to his retirement in 1986, when Consolidation closed the mines. Red was rightly proud of his sanitation role, which was essential to maintaining the clean, healthful atmosphere that characterized Coalwood.

He told me that during the peak of Coalwood's glory as a company town, a nurse traveled with him on the garbage truck. If she observed unsanitary conditions around a home or business, the responsible party was required to rectify the situation within a week or face eviction. That

The home where the Hickam family lived still stands in Coalwood. In one of his rocket experiments, Homer blew up the white picket fence that once surrounded the house.

was both the conviction and the control that mining companies exerted over its subjects.

Red was equally proud of the role that he and his truck had in helping the Rocket Boys and their teacher win the 1960 National Science Fair gold medal for their rocketry project. Red's work gave him access to materials and castoffs that the Rocket Boys used to build their rockets. Further, after completing his rounds on Saturdays, Red gave the Rocket Boys access to the trash truck for transporting construction materials to the launch site, dubbed Camp Coalwood.

We headed down the road toward the center of town, "Clubhouse Row," where the remains of shops, church, club house, and workers' apartments stood. This was the setting for the drama that unfolded in the late 1950s as Homer Hickam Jr., Quentin Wilson, Roy Lee Cooke, Sherman Siers, Jimmy "O'Dell" Carroll, and Billy Rose were coached to fame by their teacher, Freida J. Riley, who died of Hodgkin's Disease at the age of 31.

A stately white church that would be more at home in a New England town stood next to the former Club House, the roof of which provided a

Ernest Carroll loved to give tours of Coalwood to visitors and talk about the town's history and its famous Rocket Boys. His son, Jimmy, was one of them.

platform for Hickam's stargazing. Across the street was the row of shops where machinists transformed steel rods into rockets. The buildings' weathered, dilapidated condition suggested a once prosperous, sparkling community that had sputtered out like Hickam's early rockets.

"At one time, there were six mines working here in Coalwood," Red told me. "We had four stores, four schools, a barbershop, a library, and power plant. Anything that people needed, Mr. Carter (the coal company's owner and founder) saw to it that we had it." Of course, Mr. Carter owned everything, including the miners' homes, which led to an insecure lifestyle. When a miner lost his job, he also lost his home.

Beyond town, a dirt road headed off to the right at a bus shelter and disappeared into the forest. A sign painted on the simple building pointed to the "launch site." Red headed up the road to the last stop on the tour, Cape Coalwood, from which the Rocket Boys fired their increasingly powerful rockets.

A large, grassy field at the end of a rutted dirt road, the site looks nothing like that depicted in the movie, which was filmed in Tennessee,

The author with Ernest Carroll at the Coalwood crossroads, May 2004. The residents take great pride in the community's Rocket Boys fame. *Photo by Barbara Hopkins.*

not Coalwood. In the movie, Cape Coalwood is on top of a mountain, but the real Cape Coalwood is hemmed in by "Rocket Mountain." The launch pad from which Hickam and the Rocket Boys sent their science projects soaring several miles above McDowell County is long gone. But Red pointed out where the pad and shelter once stood, then took us past his house and drew our attention to his flower garden and a massive public address speaker on the hill above his property. At Christmastime, Red spun holiday records and pumped the music through that speaker for the entire neighborhood to "enjoy."

After the tour, we sat at a picnic table in the shadow of a 1950s Smokey the Bear sign and perused Red's albums filled with newspaper and magazine articles about the Rocket Boys, the movie, and Coalwood. Red said *October Sky* changed the way both the world and his hometown's residents looked at Coalwood.

"People who used to live here, until the book and movie came out, were ashamed to admit they lived here," he told me. "We all thought (the

Ernest Carroll stands on the launch pad site near the town of Coalwood. It was not on top of a mountain, as the motion picture suggests, but on this bottom land hemmed in by "Rocket Mountain."

Rocket Boys) had lost their marbles. But they proved that anything you set your heart to do, you can do it. It's just amazing that a few little boys in a little coal camp like this would get in the news and have a movie made about them. I call it a miracle."

Ernest O'Dell Carroll died at the age of 92, January 8, 2011. He had served as the Rocket Boys' Cape Coalwood tour guide for over a decade and was awarded the West Virginia 35th Star award by then Governor Joe Manchin.

Along the Way: Dave Cross #3

Coalwood's other high-profile resident in 2004 was Dave Cross #3, so numbered because "my Daddy was Dave and my Granddaddy was Dave."

He was Country Corner's equivalent of a Wal-Mart greeter. "He's the doorman," said Lyndora Hamilton, owner of the convenience store.

On sunny days, Dave parked his black SUV next to the "Welcome to Coalwood" sign at the intersection of Frog Level Road and Route 16. He stood next to his immaculately kept vehicle and waved at every motorist who passed through the busy crossing.

In Country Corner, Dave sat on the lunch bench that was closest to the entrance so he could greet each person who patronized the busy store. He started his day with a cup of coffee, bottle of Coca-Cola, and a lot of smiles.

"Seven days a week, I'm right here," said Dave, who usually arrived at the

Dave Cross waves to an acquaintance as he walks across the parking lot of Coalwood's convenience store, May 2004

store at 6:10 a.m. and stayed until the mailman made his stop there. Dave walked out to the parking lot, got his mail from the carrier, then headed home to have lunch with his mother, Catherine O'Neal.

After lunch, Dave returned to the store or his spot across the street, where he stayed until 5 p.m.

"This is my fun," the retired coal miner told me. "This is my hobby."

Chapter 12

Crazy Bear

Point Pleasant
Mason County

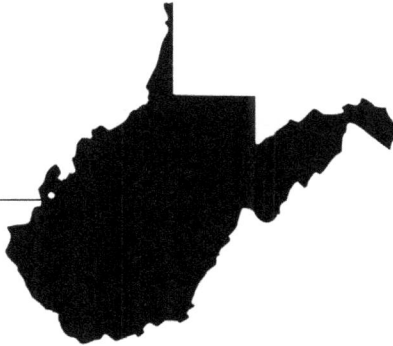

The sign on the door of Crazy Bear's Indian Store informed me that the owners no longer kept regular hours. However, because they lived just three minutes down the road, they would be happy to open the store if you would pick up the phone and dial . . .

I chose to drive down the road to the second house below the store and see if the shopkeeper, Robert "Bob" Fowler, would chat with me about his Point Pleasant landmark. He obliged and a few minutes later my wife and I were watching a demonstration of Bob's backwoods skills in a parking lot along Route 62.

Bob, known as the West Virginia Mountain Man, could split a bullet or the queen of hearts with a shot from his 22-gauge rifle fired at 20 yards. To conclude his little Annie Oakley demonstration, he nailed a playing card with his tomahawk from 25 yards, using his "bowling shot," an underhand throw.

"Overhead, backwards, straight through," Bob told me as he listed the various tomahawk moves he had mastered. "I used to throw under my leg, but my belly's gotten too big for that anymore."

During the years Bob had his Crazy Bear's store and museum, any visitor who showed an interest was treated to this demonstration of backwoods skills. During the five-minute sideshow, Bob mentioned he was national champion tomahawk thrower for three years and held the state title for 13. He also was the state's muzzle-loading champion for three consecutive years back in the 1950s.

Bob's wife Joann owned the shop, but he managed it for her because he was a perfect fit for the task: His grandmother, Ora Fowler, was part Shawnee Indian.

With a weathered face framed by a white beard and long white hair tied back in a ponytail, Bob possessed the appearance of a true mountain man rather than someone who lived just off the highway. Hanging in the store were several paintings by artist Glen Barnes, for whom Bob modeled. One of those works depicted a rugged mountaineer trudging through the snow, the kind of difficult but independent existence that Bob lived in his younger days.

He camped out in West Virginia's wildest, most remote areas and lived off the land just as his grandmother's ancestors had done. He made his own buckskin clothes, fashioned tools from rock, bone, and sticks, and ate only what he hunted or gathered.

"Anything I got a hold of," Bob said, summing up his diet during the mid-1980s winter he spent at Dolly Sods. "I learned to eat about everything, from dog on up. I've ate rattlesnake and blacksnake, but never ate copperhead."

A native of Point Pleasant, Bob attributed his interest in Native American lore to the "Straight Arrow" collector cards packed in Nabisco Shredded Wheat. Childhood fascination grew into a lifestyle.

"The Indian way of life was beautiful," Bob said. "They had a good religion. Their way of life was easy. They had their grocery store in their backyard."

Being a Boy Scout gave Bob a practical introduction to the skills he learned from Straight Arrow cards and books. He pursued this fascination in adulthood as a muzzle-loader builder and shooter, Native American artifacts collector, and hunter, trapper, fisherman, and camper.

Bob Fowler stands near the parking lot of his Crazy Bear's Indian Store, Route 62, Mason County, 2006.

In the early 1980s, Bob checked out of society and moved into the mountains.

"I was a horse auctioneer, and I was always around people. I got tired of people and decided to do it on my own," he told me. "I'd studied Indian and pioneer ways all my life. I wasn't satisfied to just read about it, I had to go out and try it for myself."

He hoped to find solitude in the wilderness, but his unusual lifestyle attracted media attention and eventually backfired on him. "Some artist, photographer would show up every time I turned around," he said.

His wife stayed behind and worked as a school bus driver to pay the bills. A combination of her displeasure with his absence and a case of pneumonia drew Bob back to civilization. He turned to making and selling wooden toys but soon discovered the market was weak in a "Star Wars" age. Next came the Shawnee Trading Post, which evolved into Crazy Bear's. "I told my wife I was going to go back into business, and she told me I was crazy if I did. She said, 'You're just like an old bear.' And I said, 'That's a good name, Crazy Bear's,'" he said.

Even with his back to the target, Bob Fowler could hit it with a shot from his firearm and a little help from a mirror.

Bob developed business relationships with many Native American tribes across North America to provide him with both prosaic and esoteric stock: blankets, rugs, jewelry, and incense; a war club made from a coyote's jaw, buffalo bone chokers, red fox heads, and the strangest item in his eclectic collection, water pails made from buffalo scrotums.

With a Buffalo Bill flair for marketing, Bob created several attractions on the grounds to keep visitors occupied while they waited, like a bin bearing a sign: "DANGER BABY RATTLERS AND COPPER HEADS."

Inside the bin, nestled in some dried leaves, are two plastic baby rattles and several pennies.

"I used to have a convex mirror out there with a sign on it that said, 'The ugliest animal in the world.' But somebody threw a brick at it and broke it," he said.

Despite his outward appearance of good humor, Bob was carrying a discouraged heart. Tourism had been way down for several years, and his wife was dealing with some serious health issues. He didn't know if Crazy Bear's would be around much longer.

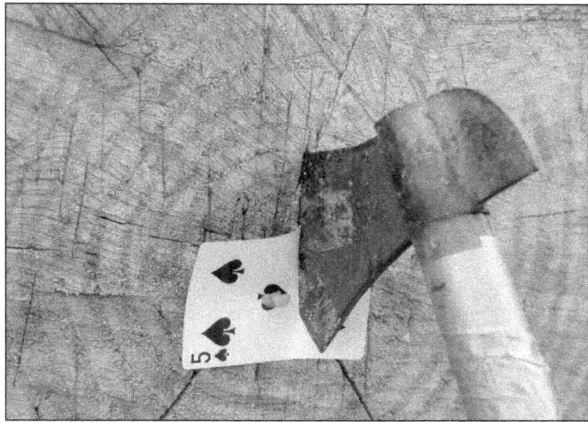

Potential buyers who stopped at Crazy Bear's store were treated to demonstrations of his backwoods skills and stories of his survival in the West Virginia wilderness. I got to believe Bob went through a lot of playing cards when his business was attracting many visitors.

He closed it for good later that summer, and as of December 2005, the couple were looking for a buyer.

Robert A. Fowler died December 19, 2010, at the age of 72. Joann, his wife of 52 years, survived him until July 2, 2013.

Paul F. Richards Sr. stumbled upon Pleasure Valley while returning from a cave-exploration trip. He maintained many of the old structures that were established by the fishing-hole attraction before he became the owner.

Chapter 12

Stumbling upon Pleasure Valley

Belington
Barbour County

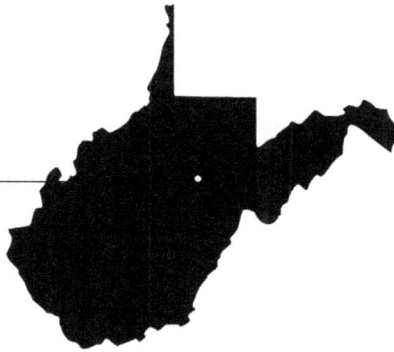

Iwas driving a relatively sporty Mazda hatchback that rode low to the
ground on soft rubber tires—not the best vehicle with which to navigate
a dirt road that soon transitioned into a trace through a meadow.

I took the road in a failed attempt to find a shortcut between Belington
in Barbour County and Montrose in Tucker County. Following my trusty
DeLorne map, I turned east on Barbour Country Road 9 and followed it
to Kirt Community, where the road to Teter Lake goes to the right and the
narrow byway to Montrose takes a left. The map didn't indicate that this
"road" becomes a gravel path engulfed by a forested valley. Eventually, the
glorified cow path delivered my father and I to an unplanned destination,
Pleasure Valley Trout Farm.

The farm appeared to be frozen in time, and I was soon interviewing
its owner, Paul F. Richards Sr., whose first interaction with this place also
came about by accident.

Hand-lettered signage posted on a rustic building served the Pleasure Valley enterprise for many years. Owner Paul Richards waits for the next fisherman.

Paul and his wife, Kathleen, were visiting the area from Clarksburg one weekend, and they took the road from Route 219 to avoid road construction. Paul, a spelunker, had been exploring limestone caves in the region when he came upon the back road.

"We got to the top of a hill, and it was hot, and we had the windows rolled down," Paul said. "We could hear this church music playing about halfway down."

The music reassured the couple that they were near civilization, and they followed the holy strains to a mom-and-pop roadside attraction consisting of a very small snack shop, picnic pavilion, and two ponds stocked with goldfish and trout.

Paul and Kathleen had arrived in Pleasure Valley.

"We stopped and seen that they had pop and stuff," Paul said. "We got something cold to drink, and the old fellow who had it asked if we'd like to see the fish, so I bought a bag of food and fed them."

The old man, who Paul recalled as Aldine Poling, asked what drew the

Paul Richards tries his hand at fishing in one of the ponds at his Pleasure Valley.

couple to his valley. When he learned that Paul was a cave explorer, he told him about a dandy limestone cave up the road.

"He told me you could feel this cold air coming out of the sink, and there was a room in there with a big flat rock. The men from around here would go up there and sit with their lanterns and play cards to get away from their women," Paul said.

Paul made a mental note of the cave and promised he'd explore it someday. Nearly two years passed before he returned, only to discover that Aldine had died and that his widow was looking for a buyer. Drawn to the peaceful setting, nearby caves, and retirement potential of the property, Paul and Kathleen purchased it in 1969 and made it their home. For 25 years, Paul made the 100-mile commute to his job in Clarksburg. But he never explored the fabled cave that offered local married men a respite from domestic miseries. Road construction and blasting in the area evidently collapsed the grotto's ceiling.

After retiring from Lockheed Martin, Paul went full time on the trout farm. He reconfigured the ponds to stock trout in one of them and a mix of bass, catfish, perch, carp, Koi, and others in a second. A Laurel Mountain spring fed the trout pond. At one time, the farm raised the fish that swim in these ponds, but by 2015, Paul was stocking about a thousand pounds of farm fish weekly.

Through word of mouth and a few motorists seeking a shortcut, Paul built up a faithful clientele of fishermen and their families.

"I got people coming in from 17 different states," he said. "I got regulars who make it a habit to come here."

The farm operated seven days a week and in all kinds of weather; determined fishermen turned to ice fishing in the winter. "I've had as many as seven holes in the ice and 14 people on there at one time. I had five to six people, taking their turn, lined up at one hole where the fish were hitting."

Vestiges of the farm's 1950s-roadside attraction days included three scaled-down structures: a white frame church with a steeple, an open display case, and a small shed. The buildings were repositories for all manner of artifacts: rocks containing fossils, rusty roller skates, a small crocodile, a stuffed bobcat, and old pots and pans. "He had them there for people to look at," Paul said. "Over the years, people have abused the things."

Except for the church: Its door opened to reveal a Nativity scene, ceramic-figure church choir, and pews. Figurines and salt-and-pepper shakers deposited there by 1960s Sunday-afternoon visitors lined the church windows. On the front of the church, just below the eaves, was the loudspeaker that once reproduced the recorded church music that originally drew Paul and Kathleen to the valley. Paul continued the tradition of playing sacred music after he and his wife acquired the property.

"I had some people complain about the music," he told me. "When the equipment went bad, I never bothered to replace it."

A plaque near the church once credited Aldine Poling as the founder of Pleasure Valley. Paul saw no need to change the place's name; surrounded by hills and wildlife, this valley was indeed a pleasurable place for Paul Richards and those who stumbled upon it.

"Everything is a lot quieter and slower around here than in the major cities," Paul said.

Although I am not one to enjoy fishing, Pleasure Valley prompted a bit of déjà vu. I was certain I'd been there as a child with my maternal grandparents, Clayton and Violet Keiper Watring. They were both deceased, so I could not confirm the prior visit. But the little chapel's windowsills filled with knickknacks whispered, "Welcome back, my wanderer," and

Old stuff collected and displayed in the little buildings at Pleasure Valley recalled a time when tourists' expectations were minimal and just getting away for a Sunday drive was recreation enough. The figures in the top photo were in the little church and brought back memories of my grandmother's penchant for knickknacks.

convinced me that Violet had contributed a bauble or two for me to discover in my travels.

I visited Pleasure Valley in 2002. More than 20 years later, the mom-and-pop attraction was still in business with Paul at the helm. Paul celebrated his 50th anniversary of ownership in 2019. His wife, Kathleen, died May 28, 2020, at their Pleasure Valley home. She was 89. Paul survived her.

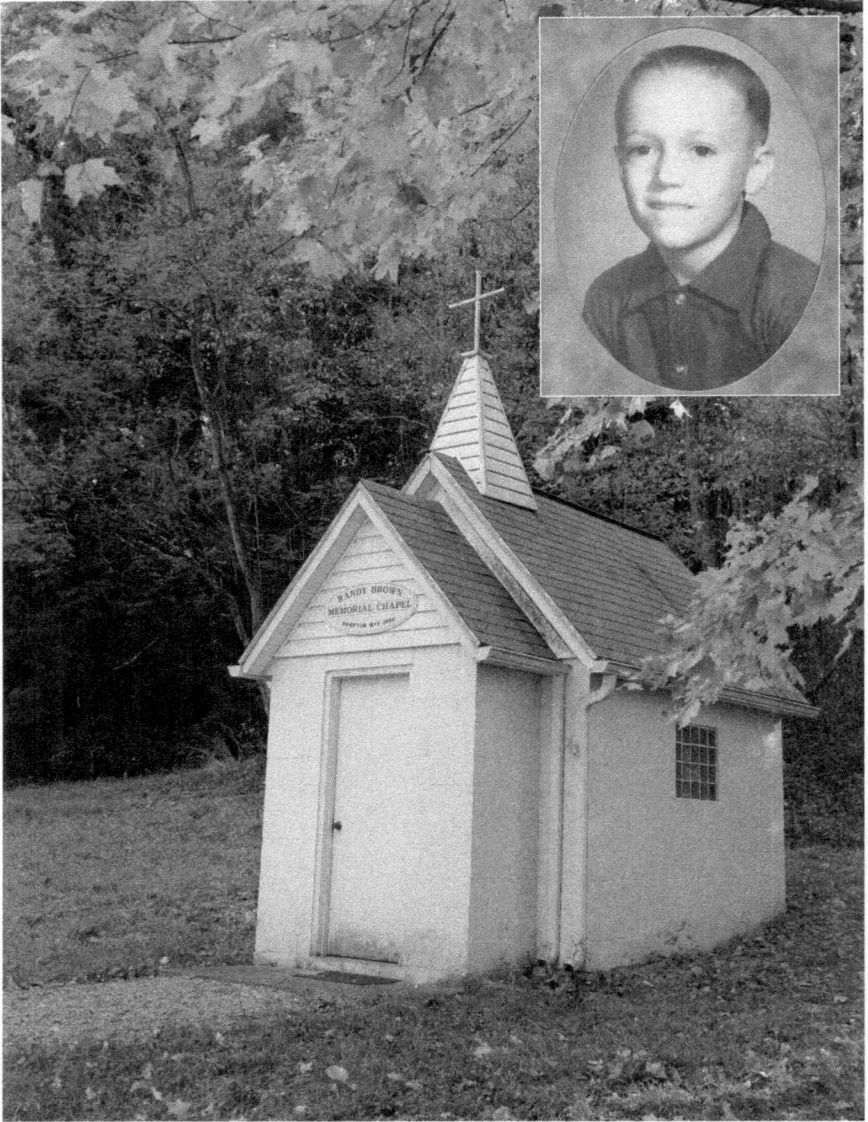

The Randy Brown Memorial Chapel is located at the intersection of Route 20 and Sago Road, south of Buckhannon. The chapel is a memorial to its namesake child, who died at the age 7. These kinds of discoveries usually end up in more back-roads wanderings as I try track down the people behind the story.
Inset photo of Randy Brown from the chapel.

Chapter 13

Chapel for a Little Boy

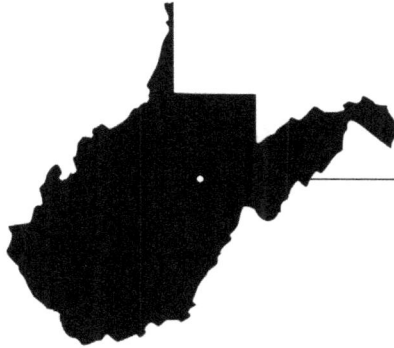

Sago
Upshur County

It stands on a wooded knoll, just off the Sago Road that leads to the site of the January 2, 2006, Upshur County mining disaster that took the lives of 12 miners.

The sign on the little chapel reads: "Randy Brown Memorial Chapel, Hampton MYF 1966." Immediately inside the door of this steeple-topped miniature chapel hangs a faded color portrait of Randy Brown, who died in 1965 at the age of 7.

The chapel interior is plain—white walls; four short, simple, low pews facing a slightly elevated platform, and a simple pulpit upon which rests an open Bible. A few children's books are scattered across the front pew. A window made of glass blocks arranged in the shape of a cross is embedded in the front wall. Glass-block windows on each side of the wall admit whatever sunlight filters through the overhanging branches.

A poem was tacked above a podium toward the rear of the chapel and oversaw the registration book. The signatures therein documented a steady stream of visitors, local and distant, whose visits to the chapel and adjoining Childrens Memorial Park raised more questions than answers. Who was Randy Brown? What claimed him at such a young age? What was so special about his life that it compelled those around him to erect this wayside memorial?

A few miles down the road, Ron Hinkle, a glass artisan who has lived on the family farm all his life, helped unravel the mystery. Randy was his second-grade classmate at Hampton School.

"I can still remember when someone came knocking on the schoolhouse door," Ron recalled. "The teacher came in and gave us the news that Randy had passed away."

Ron's memory of his classmate is one of a sickly boy who missed a lot of school because of illness and surgeries. A half century had erased details, however. He also lost track of Randy's parents, Archie "Bud" and Marlene Brown, but was positive that they were still alive and living in the Hampton house where Randy grew up.

I followed the tip and got lost. Eventually, neighbors told me that Bud and Marlene moved years ago, but after a few phone calls, I located Randy's adopted brother, Charles Brown, a French Creek resident who pointed me to his father.

Bud Brown lived on Truby's Run, off Truckers' Lane, south of Buckhannon. Marlene, Bud's first wife and Randy's mother, died in 2004. Bud struggled to recall the details of Randy's life, but his memory of his only biological son is vivid and bittersweet.

"Randy, he was very quiet," Bud told me. "Randy and me, we were real close. He was more or less a daddy's boy. He always went out and helped me work. He thought he was a mechanic and wanted to help me work on cars."

Bud's job at the time was driving a charter bus. The trips were mostly local, but occasionally he'd make the Clarksburg-to-Wheeling overnighter and Randy accompanied him.

"He'd sit up there in the front seat right across from me," Bud said. "He thought he was a big man."

Randy liked school, but his greatest pleasure was being around his father and acting grownup. Perhaps that was important to Randy because his span on this sphere was to be so short. Bud said their son had a kidney that did not function from birth, but the defect went undetected until Randy became gravely ill.

The chapel interior is plain with an open Bible on the pulpit and four short, wooden pews without padding. Assorted children's books are spread across one of the pews. A few minutes in the chapel will make any visitor grateful for his life and health, regardless of age.

"He was very active," Bud said. "He went to school and was very active. We didn't know it for a long time, and then he just got sick. He kept getting worse. They did this operation and that operation on him."

Bud said complications set in after their son's damaged kidney was removed, and he never recovered.

"My mother used to tell me about the times he was in (the hospital) at Morgantown for six weeks at a time, and (Marlene) would go there and stay the whole time," Charles Brown told me.

Randy was buried in Hampton Cemetery, across from the United Methodist Church where he was a member of the MYF.

Bud said that group and its sponsoring church erected the chapel a year after Randy died. The St. Clair family provided the land. Oral Starkey and Cecil Linger, members of the church, designed the chapel and assisted other volunteers in building it. Memorial donations paid for the materials.

Maintaining it was another matter. For several summers, Ron Hinkle

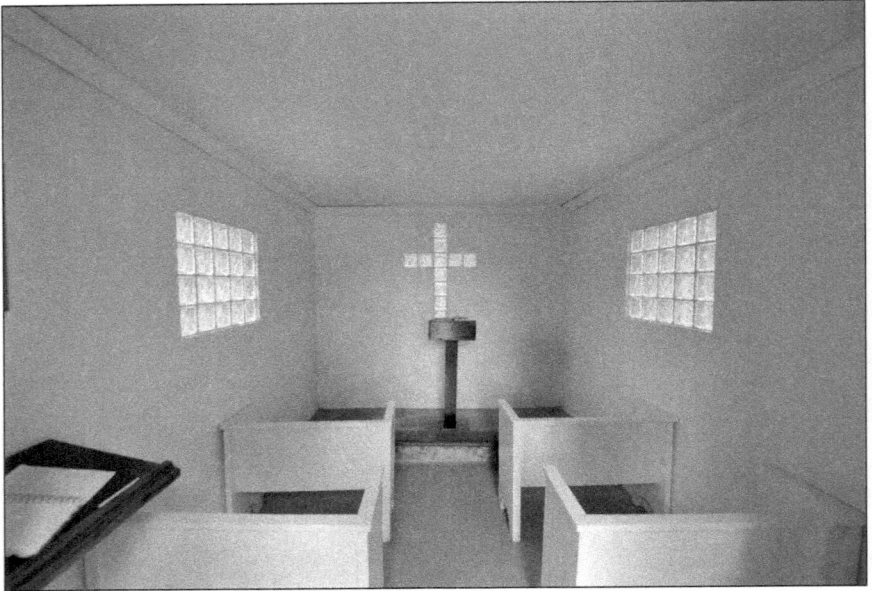

A cross made of glass blocks provides a symbol of hope in this chapel to a little boy, Randy Brown.

and his son cared for the property, which doubles as a memorial park for area children. Volunteers from the church helped, as well as Bud and Charles. Bud had a bad heart and couldn't do what once did down there. That bothered him, a lot.

Bud enjoyed going to the chapel to remember his all-grown-up son and the wonderful times they had. On Christmas Day, 2006, Charles honored the brother he never knew—he was adopted after Randy died—when he chose the chapel for the site of his wedding ceremony. He and Kirsten Chapman walked down the short aisle on Christmas Day 2006.

"We had 17 people there," Charles told me. "We actually all didn't fit in there, but it was close."

Along the Way: Sago Mine Disaster Memorial

On January 2, 2006, the little Upshur County town of Sago captured the nation's attention and heart as rescue workers tried to save the lives of 13 coal miners trapped about 2 miles inside the mine.

One miner was killed in the explosion and 12 others attempted to find sanctuary from the poisonous atmosphere. It took rescuers 44 hours to reach the men; by that time, only one miner remained alive, Randal L. McCloy Jr., 26. The disaster received widespread media coverage, some of which initially provided incorrect information about the trapped miners' wellbeing. The false hopes were dashed when the men were finally reached.

One of the names on the memorial is Jesse Jones, whose brother, Owen Mark, also worked at the Sago mine. Owen had been assigned to another crew that entered the mine about 10 minutes behind the doomed miners. He assisted other rescue workers in the futile attempt to reach his brother and the others. Owen eventually left the Sago Mine and went to work at the Pleasant Hill Mine near Mill Creek. In August 2017, Owen Jones died in that mine, leaving behind a wife, two children, and five grandchildren.

The brothers' great grandfather also had died in a coal mining incident.

Sago Mine was the worst disaster of its kind in West Virginia since the 1968 Farmington No. 9 Mine explosion that claimed 78 lives. Four years and three months after the Sago Mine Disaster, 29 West Virginia miners were killed in a coal dust explosion at the Upper Big Branch Mine in Raleigh County. In all three disasters, inquiries determined that lax safety practices had contributed to the disasters.

Sometimes when I need to add a little heat to my writing corner or fire up the computer to design a book or edit a video, I think about the sacrifices that coalminers make so we can have the energy and steel we take for granted (much of the coal mined in this region is metallurgical). Extracting this mineral requires men of great courage, and children somewhere still grieve for their fathers whose lives ended prematurely because society expects such comforts and materials.

Chapter 14

Reed's Mill on Second Creek

Gap Mills
Monroe County

Spend an hour or two shelling corn and chewing the fat with Larry Mustain at his Reed's Mill, and the conversation eventually gets around to sex.

"We heard a bunch of splashing by that little bridge (over the mill raceway)," Larry told me on a sunny October day in 2021. "I go over to where I could see what was making the noise, and it was two turtles. I think they were having sex; they were all locked up, as they say. They floated down (the raceway), and I kept thinking, 'Where are they going?' They went right over the spillway, locked up."

Locking up—or, more accurately, the results of it—is a frequent a topic at this mill, along with the weather, politics, and Bloody Butcher cornmeal recipes. Larry is the go-to genealogist and historian of this bucolic farming valley in northern Monroe County. Larry's paternal great, great grandfather Thomas Mustain settled in the area circa 1840; the Reeds, his maternal side of the family, have been there for three generations. Fall Reed, his grandfather, was associated with several Second Creek mills; Clara Reed, Fall's wife, ran the Second Creek Post Office from the 1920s to 1947. Larry was born in the circa 1900 mill house down the road.

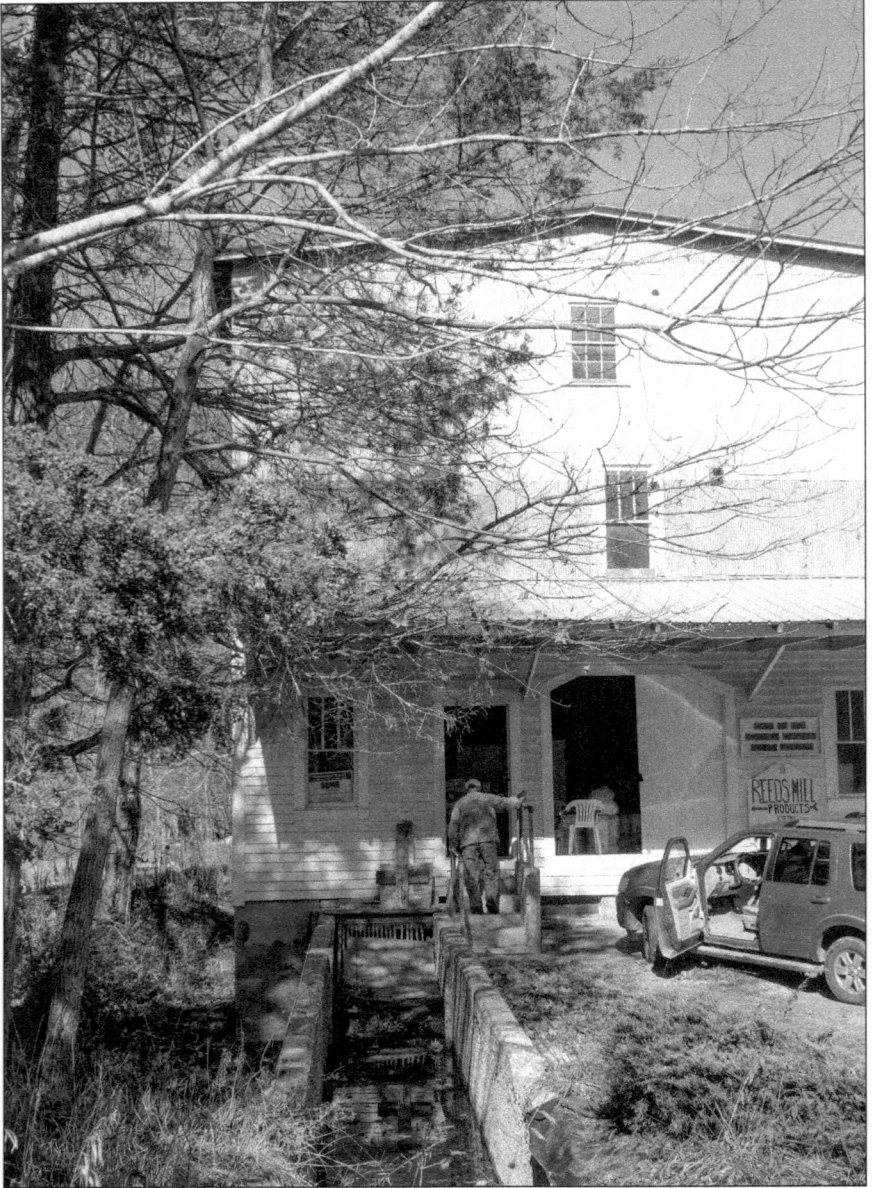

Larry Mustain arrives at Reed's Mill for another day of shelling and grinding corn, just as his maternal family members did for year. The mill no longer operates on water power although it is along Second Creek, a stream that hosted as many as 20 mills at one time, said Larry, the resident historian of Gap Mills.

As Larry told me that day, "You could make a career of Second Creek (history)," and he has done that. Thus, while old-timers from the region still purchase their open-pollinated cornmeal at Reed's, first-timers typically discover the place in their quest for ancestral information, the whereabouts of an old family farm, or directions to the Highland Park Church Cemetery.

Those seeking the "tourist attraction" promised on the highway sign along Route 219 discover a classic water-powered grist mill and a broom factory, both idled because of circumstances beyond Larry's control. Lacking a water wheel and standing some distance from the creek that powers it, the white frame building bears little resemblance to the mill at Babcock State Park or Cook's Mill, a distant cousin in the same county. "Most of our old mills around here are just for show," Larry said. "They are tourist attractions, and this is, too, in a way."

Only Reed's and the long-closed Roger's Mill, which is in considerably worse condition, remain of the nearly two-dozen mills that once took their power from Second Creek. Fed by the springs of Peter's Mountain to the southeast, the stream falls 600 feet as it travels from its headwaters to Reed's Mill on Second Creek Road. Larry said settlers harnessed this free source of energy that rambles through northern Monroe and southern Greenbrier counties.

"Second Creek has never gone dry," Larry said, drawing upon the anecdotes of family members who worked in mills along the creek. "The driest time in running the mill was 1932; they went from May to October with very little rain, but the creek never went dry. But it got to the point where (the miller) could only grind for one hour, then have to wait for the head to fill back up."

This reliable flow hosted gristmills, sawmills, two woolen mills, and a powder mill. The latter manufactured gunpowder from charcoal, sulfur, and saltpeter, which was mined in a cave on the former Dickson farm. The powder mill was the first to go, literally.

"(The owner) was in the house at dark and he needed his glasses," Larry told me. "He realized he'd left them in the powder mill, so he sent his slave and her child out to get them. Not thinking that she was in a powder mill, she lit a candle. The mill blew up and killed both (the slave and her child). It was rebuilt . . . the owner went in one night to do something in it, and it blew up, killing the owner."

Larry Mustain loves to talk Gap Mills and Second Creek history and geneal-
ogy with those who stop for a look around the mill. His hours are mostly by
appointment.

According to the pamphlet Larry hands each first-time visitor, Reed's
Mill was built in 1791 by Archibald McDowell, who owned thousands of
acres in this area. Larry's family, long associated with the farming valley,
took ownership of the mill in 1914. Larry's familial tie is through his late
mother, "Birdie" Marie Reed, whose brother Aubrey Francis Reed became
owner in 1925.

Aubrey Reed, whose epitaph honors him as "A Second Creek Miller in
the Gap Mills Tradition," was born October 12, 1904, and died September
29, 1989. Larry speaks reverently of the man who owned both the mill and
over 300 acres of farmland on which he grew many of the grains processed
at the mill.

"My uncle was such a character. He had a third-grade education, and
I'm totally prejudiced when I say this, but he was the smartest man I ever
knew. He never went to church, but he also was the most religious man
I've ever known," Larry said.

Like Larry's mother, Aubrey also was a Democrat, a political anomaly
in both the family and valley.

"My mother could look at you and tell whether you were a Republican

Larry Mustain as a child with his uncle Aubrey Reed. Larry learned the art of milling under his uncle's guidance and became the mill's owner after Aubrey passed. Larry was concerned about what would become of this family treasure, the last mill on Second Creek, when he departs this life.

Photo from Larry Mustain collection

or Democrat. By the time I went away to college, I realized it was prejudice. Any person who was wearing a three-piece suit and had a bit of a belly had to be a Republican," said Larry, who carries on the Reed family tradition as "Roosevelt-Truman-Johnson-Obama Democrats." "All the Reeds were Republicans, except on my mother's side, and they were so radical," he said.

To prove his point, Larry tells of that time when a presidential aide to Dwight Eisenhower showed up at the mill to purchase some yellow cornmeal for the chef at The Greenbrier, where the Republican president was on a golf outing. Eisenhower had requested cornbread made from stone-ground yellow corn.

"My uncle had the grinder going and told the man he was grinding white corn that day," Larry said, recounting the story that was written by an Associated Press reporter. "The guy said, 'But, it's for the president.' And my uncle said, 'I don't care who it is for.'"

Second Creek once had sufficient flow to power several mills. These days, the stream is much more valuable as a recreational resource that draws visitors to Greenbrier and Monroe counties, two of the author's favorite back-roads haunts.

Larry said his uncle told the man he planned to grind yellow corn the next day, and the man requested that Aubrey deliver a bag to the Greenbrier's kitchen. "And my uncle said, 'I don't deliver to anybody.' But, if (Eisenhower) had been a Democrat, he would ground it and delivered it for him," Larry said.

Last mill on Second Creek

Larry, born October 25, 1936, came under the care of his Uncle Aubrey when Larry's father, Emory Parker Mustain, became ill in 1942. Emory had gone to Charleston during the war and contracted a life-threatening illness resulting from exposure to toxins at the chemical plant where he worked. "It took four years to get straightened out from that," Larry said.

While under Aubrey's care, Larry worked as a farm and mill hand for his uncle.

Larry Mustain, owner of Reed's Mill, takes a well-earned break from his labors as a miller, which involves much physical labor just to keep a supply of water to the turbines.

"I'd been raised here, and I'd helped him ever since I was a kid," Larry said. "I shelled corn and stuff from the time I was in third or fourth grade."

Larry moved to Newport News, Virginia, at the age of 16. He met there his late wife Frances, also a staunch Democrat, reared four children, and worked as a teacher and school principal from Virginia to California. In 1975, he returned to Second Creek to help his uncle with the mill and farm.

"As they say, absence makes the heart grow fonder, so I had to come back," Larry told me. "I just wanted the mill to stay in the family."

The times had changed, however, and with those changes came impossible challenges for a small, water-powered mill like Reed's. Larry said several other mills were still operating on Second Creek when he was a youth. They included:

■ Clark's Mill, a taller structure than Reed's and operated by his Grandfather Reed. The dam washed away in a 1968 flood, and the mill buildings were destroyed in the 1970s;

■ The Red Mill, now gone, was near Gap Mills and operated by his Grandmother Reed's uncle, Oscar Neel;

■ Roger's Mill, which still stands and dates from the 1770s;

■ Nickell Mill, built in 1814 and, despite being on the National Register of Historic Places, was torn down in the past decade.

The latter mill ceased operation in 1949, the same year Aubrey Reed gave his operation a makeover. Aubrey enclosed the front porch to create an office area and made operational upgrades. Fortunately, he retained soon-to-be-antiquated equipment such as the American Midget Marvel. The Marvel is a self-contained roller mill that was produced by the Anglo American Mill Co. of Owensboro, Kentucky. It offered small gristmills the flexibility of producing a "better barrel of flour cheaper." Larry said Aubrey installed the equipment in 1926.

"We used it to make white flower, wheat, whole wheat flour, buckwheat, bran, and graham," Larry said. It was last run in the 1970s, but Larry keeps it and other antiquated mill equipment as artifacts of milling history.

The mill's waterwheel, however, is long gone, replaced with twin turbines circa 1880. They operate in 10 feet of water below the milling floor; each turbine is capable of 10 horsepower. The turbines power the millstones and drive the mill's legacy machinery, such as the grain elevator, roller mill, feed mixer, and bagger.

"We could grind about 100 pounds an hour," Larry said. "It all depends on what you're grinding. Up until two years ago, this whole mill was run off 20 horsepower of water."

Aubrey's operation focused on dairy feed when Larry came back in 1975, but Larry saw the mill's future in offering consumers stone-ground flour and cornmeal ground from the open-pollinated grains grown on the family farm.

Larry worked alongside Aubrey, learning the miller's craft and preparing himself for the responsibility of being the third Reed family member to own and operate the mill. He said people in the valley suspected he'd moved back just to get access to the land and his uncle's money.

"But it was exactly the opposite of that," Larry said. "We never talked about specifics when I moved back. Once, when we were bailing hay, he said to me, 'I'm going to give you this farm.' And I said, 'No, I don't want you to do that. I said fix it so I can buy it because he lived there with his sister (and family) at the mill house, and I told him did not need to worry about (taking care of her), also.'"

Equipment once used to fill large sacks with the milled grain has not been operated in decades. Flour and cornmeal customers buy small quantities for home use, not 50-pound bags for making moonshine!

Mucky situation

Whatever he inherited, Larry got it through hard labor, such as shoveling knee-deep mud from the turbine box into buckets and hauling them away. "My uncle told me (as Larry shoveled), "That is the glory of waterpower," Larry said.

For a man in the process of completing his ninth decade, however, the glory became a curse and perhaps the mill's sunset. Larry told me that the reason the mill had not used waterpower since 2018 is because mud choked the holding pond and raceway. A dam diverts water from Second Creek into the holding pond above the mill, but without periodic flooding that otherwise would have flushed mud from the pond, it became a fertile, stagnant basin for plant life.

"There's something going on with the creek there that I don't understand," Larry said. "We used to live on fish out of that creek from February to July when I was a kid. There is some kind of algae in it now, some kind of plant that looks like seaweed that makes the pond fill up faster."

Before Larry could fire up those turbines, the 6-foot-deep deposit of muck and organic debris would have to be cleared from pond. It would require a contractor with a backhoe and dump truck to accomplish the work. While he received a small grant to clean out the pond and race, Larry needed much more funding to accomplish all the tasks necessary to restore waterpower operation to the mill. The turbines need to be rebuilt and the millstones groomed before the mill can once again operate under waterpower from Second Creek. The mill building itself needs a refresh and treatment for powder post beetles.

To satisfy the regional demand for special cornmeal and flours, Larry resorted to using an electrical stone grinder. "We're grinding with a portable upright grinder. My uncle would never use it because it heats the grain, and he said it changed the taste of the cornbread a little bit," Larry said. "All he would use were the two big stones run by waterpower. But I haven't used them for three years now."

His mainstay product is Bloody Butcher cornmeal, an open-pollinated variety with a history reaching back to the Native American occupants of this land. His grandfather and uncle once grew the variety on the bottom land; Larry relies upon another farmer for this corn, the ears of which can

Bloody butcher corn is one of the open-pollinated grains that Larry grinds at his Second Creek mill. With the mill pond full of muck, Larry has turned to grinding with an electric device; his Uncle Aubrey would not approve.

be red, speckled, purple, orange, or white. He claims that these native grains are hardier, higher in antioxidants, and have more bran content than the non-GMO hybrids that large-scale food producers use for their meals. He also offers buckwheat, once grown on the Reed farm but now sourced from an outside supplier because wild turkeys kept decimating his plantings.

"It's gotten to where the only thing we can raise here is hay," Larry said of the valley's farmland. "In the past two years, we had two seven-acre patches of corn, and the bears ate it all."

Larry grinds and bags small batches of meal and flour, then stores them in several refrigerators so the product is always available for his regular customers. The quantities are small; it has been years since he's needed the old Stowe bagger that could fill 25-pound sacks of flour. Reed's Mill has not had orders of that magnitude for decades.

Larry said one of Aubrey's customers purchased 400 to 500 pounds of cornmeal at a time, a quantity indicative of a clandestine application.

"He makes big pans of cornbread . . . he's bound to be making bread with it," Aubrey would tell Larry, all the while knowing the buyer had a more profitable use for the grain.

"The old guy's father was running a still, and they were putting the stuff in plastic milk jugs," said Larry, who asked his uncle about the client's choice of containers, given alcohol's solvent property.

"My uncle said, 'Don't worry about that. It's not going to sit around in a jug that damned long,'" Larry said.

In 2024, Larry needs a few big orders from moonshiners. In prior years, his annual flour and cornmeal sales have amounted to only two grand, hardly enough to keep the lights and certainly not a profitable legacy for his four children, 10 grandchildren, and 26 great-grandchildren. Family members assist him as their time allows, but Larry knows the value of his place is in the land, not its past or the buckwheat flour that "mostly older people want because everybody ate buckwheat cakes from the winter to early spring," as Larry said.

As of early 2024, the mill was open by request and chance. Since losing his wife several years ago, it has become a mainstay in his social life, as well as therapy and something a man rarely gets in his graying days: An opportunity to connect to and perpetuate a family legacy, even if he's the last man standing.

"I keep thinking I should quit," Larry told me as I packed up my gear and headed out for more wanderings. "My saying is: "19 down and one to go, meaning there were (at least) 20 mills on Second Creek and 19 of them are gone. And now, maybe it's my turn."

Along the Way: An Old Broom Factory

The back room of Reed's Mill houses the Everett Hogsett broom factory, named for the 19th-century Second Creek resident who started the enterprise.

Everett, who had five sisters and three brothers, was born Nov. 9, 1859. His parents were Hiram McElhaney Hogshead (Hogsett) and Mary Jane Miller Hogsett.

Up until the late 1930s, Everett owned most of the land that comprises the Reed's Mill farm and one-room schoolhouse property. Cannonballs were occasionally plowed up on the Hogsett farm, and Larry suspected that they were evidence of a Battle of Second Creek. But Everett told Larry that men from the area who were too old to join the army secured a cannon to protect their homes and farms in the event of a Yankee or Confederate invasion. They practiced firing the cannon across the field that would become the Mustain farm but never had to go to battle with it!

Everett became a broom maker, acquiring equipment manufactured in Schenectady, New York, prior to the Civil War. Larry says the six machines in the workroom facilitate the manufacture of a broom from the raw materials of wood, twine, and the broom corn grown on the farm.

One of the machines removes the seeds from the thin strands of the annual grass called millet, sorghum, or broom corn. Strands are cut to a uniform length and wrapped around the handle, producing a round broom with its bristles attached to the handle with wire. From there, a foot-powered vise is used to flatten the broom. Shakers are credited with inventing the machinery that transforms the round broom into a flat one, believed to be more efficient at its job. The flattened broom is stitched with several rows of cord in the final step in this human-powered process.

Paul Nichols was the second person to operate the factory, the equipment from which was purchased by Jim Rose after Nichols' passing. Jack Fissori was the most recent broom maker to conduct the business. Fissori was manufacturing whisk, children's, hearth, utility, and full-sized brooms as recently as 2013.

Larry Mustain told me that a broom maker would challenged to find a domestic source for the materials that go into the once ubiquitous tool.

"We used to raise our own broom corn here on the farm," Larry said. "Now, there is hardly anyone in the United States raising broom corn."

A skilled craftsman equipped with the right materials could walk into the shop, brush off the equipment, and start making brooms. With an endless supply of flour dust and chaff produced in the adjoining mill, the broom artisan would be assured of at least one customer at the last mill standing on Second Creek, Monroe County.

Bibliography

The author conducted in-person interviews with all of the sources quoted in this work. These interviews provide the bulk of the text. Most of these people are no longer with us.

Dates of passing were obtained through online obituary sources, including newspapers, funeral home websites, and the Find-a-grave website.

Background information was drawn from a variety of sources, with the primary resource being the West Virginia Humanities Council's 2006 *The West Virginia Encyclopedia.* The online resource version of the same also was consulted.

Index

Carl and back-roads traveling companion, Edison, a rescue.

Carl E. Feather is a seventh-generation Preston County, West Virginia, resident; his fourth great-grandparents, Jacob and Mary Feather (Vätter), settled in the county in 1803. The story of his German-Swiss Palatinate immigrant ancestors and their relationship to the Allegheny Mountains is told in *My Fathers' Land,* also by Carl. His book, *Mountain People in a Flat Land* (Ohio University Press), relates the story of migration from West Virginia to Ohio in the post-World War II years.

Carl is married to Ruth Evans Feather, a Certified Ophthalmic Technician originally from eastern Pennsylvania. Carl and Ruth have been Bruceton Mills, West Virginia, residents since 2020.

A retired journalist and professional photographer, Carl has freelanced for West Virginia's traditional life magazine, *GOLDENSEAL,* since the mid-1980s, and more than 100 of his stories have been published in its pages. He continues to write and photograph for the quarterly. His Backroads feature has been a staple of the magazine since 2004.

Wander more West Virginia Back Roads

If you enjoyed this book, please consider other titles in this series, as well as *My Fathers' Land,* and Carl's books about another aspect of Appalachia—Ashtabula County, Ohio. All books in this series are available from our online bookstore, Books.by/feather-cottage-media.

To subscribe to *GOLDENSEAL* magazine, visit the West Virginia Department of Arts, Culture & History website: https://wvculture.org/discover/publications/goldenseal/.

Other books in this series:
More Wandering Back-Roads West Virginia
Even More Wandering Back-Roads West Virginia
Still More Wandering Back-Roads West Virginia
Wandering Tucker County, West Virginia (2025)
Wandering Route 50 West Virginia (2026)
(all with Carl E. Feather)

As an independent author and publisher, reviews are our lifeline to gaining new readers.
Please support our work by reviewing this book at
amazon.com
good reads.com.

Booksellers: We would love to have you stock our independently published books. Please send your inquiry to
carl@thefeathercottage.com.

Order Feather Cottage Media books online at

books.by/feather-cottage-media

www.ingramcontent.com/pod-product-compliance
Lightning Source LLC
Chambersburg PA
CBHW061321110426
42742CB00012BA/2274